MOVING MOUNTAINS

An integrative manual to help youth with intensity, reactivity, and anxiety

Marit E. Appeldoorn
MSW, LICSW, RPT-S

Kathy Flaminio
MSW, LGSW, ERYT-200

1000 Petals, LLC
Saint Paul, Minnesota

Copyright © 2020, 2021, Marit E. Appeldoorn and Kathy Flaminio. All rights reserved.
Cover photograph © 2008, 2020 Nancy Chakrin Photography
All rights reserved. No part of this publication may be reproduced, stored in any retrieval system, or transmitted in any form or by any means, electronic, mechanical, photocopying, recording, scanning, or other wise, without written permission from the authors.

Published by:
1000 Petals, LLC

IntegrativeTherapyMN.com
MAppeldoornLICSW@gmail.com
www.safehavenmn.com
Move-Mindfully.com
kathy@move-mindully.com

ISBN: 9780998776422
Second edition, 2021
LCCN: 2020903294

Edited by Marly Cornell, animarly@aol.com
Graphic illustrations and design by Jane Eyestone, jane.eyestone@gmail.com
Design and production by Dorie McClelland, dorie@springbookdesign.com
Cover photograph by Nancy Chakrin Photography, nancy@nancychakrin.com
Author photographs by Jake Armour, jake@armourphoto.com

Printed in the USA by Bookmobile.

This manual is for all the youth who bravely walk a difficult path,
and for all the adults who strive to be alongside them every step of the way.

CONTENTS

FOREWORD vii

INTRODUCTION viii

    WHY DO WE CALL THIS AN "INTEGRATIVE" MANUAL? ix

    HOW TO USE THIS MANUAL x

THE FOUNDATION 1

    WHAT DO WE SEE? 5

    ENVIRONMENTAL PATHWAYS 9

    INTERNAL/ORGANIC PATHWAYS 11

    IMPACT AND OUTCOMES 13

THE MOUNTAIN: A FRAMEWORK TO UNDERSTAND WHAT'S HAPPENING 19

    THE FOOTHILLS 23

        CASE STUDY: MICHAEL 23

        STRATEGIES THAT WORK 25

    THE TREELINE 35

        CASE STUDY: SARAH 35

        INTERVENTIONS 37

        STRATEGIES THAT WORK 38

THE SNOWLINE 48

    CASE STUDY: TANYA 50

    CASE STUDY: MICHAEL 52

    STRATEGIES THAT WORK 54

WHAT'S IN YOUR BACKPACK? 61

    HOW TO USE THIS SECTION 62

    FEELINGS IN THE BODY 63

    SENSORY THRESHOLDS 66

    TEMPERAMENT 70

CONCLUSION 73

    WHAT ARE THE NEXT STEPS? 74

APPENDICES 75

    GLOSSARY 76

    BIBLIOGRAPHY, RESOURCES 79

    WORKSHEETS 81

WHO WE ARE: MARIT AND KATHY 90

FOREWORD

Mental health disorders are increasingly common conditions of childhood. One of every five teens in America has a mental health disorder,[1] while one of every six children has been diagnosed with a neurodevelopmental problem such as autistic spectrum disorder, learning disabilities, ADHD, etc.[2] It is no exaggeration to say that we are facing a mental health crisis.

I have been a practicing psychiatrist for thirty years, and I am convinced that the way out of this crisis is not through more pills, but rather through better skills. The skills needed are not magic nor mysterious. They are the sort of skills that help ground the nervous system and make difficult emotions more manageable. They are readily taught and more easily learned in childhood than in adulthood. Children desperately need those kinds of skills, and such skills need to be widely accessible.

The *Moving Mountains* manual is devoted to this endeavor and, with Marit Appeldoorn and Kathy Flaminio, we are blessed with very able guides. Everyone needs the ability to calm their own nervous system and regulate their own emotions to cope more or less successfully with their own life challenges and stresses, which are not likely to become any easier any time soon. Use the ideas in this manual, come back to them often, learn them, teach them, and together let's aim to ease this escalating suffering at least a little bit.

—Henry Emmons, MD, author of *The Chemistry of Joy* and *The Chemistry of Calm*

For the past twenty-three years that I have practiced and taught adolescent medicine, it has been clear to me that one of the greatest health challenges for children and adolescents is maintaining an optimal state of mental health as they grow up. They face so many challenges in their worlds. They do not always have the guidance or opportunity to develop the social and emotional skills to manage negative emotions and cope with the smaller and the bigger stresses of life. *Moving Mountains* offers a compelling approach for parents and other adults caring for children and adolescents. Contained within is a vivid framework that is imaginative, informative, and highly practical. Kathy Flaminio and Marit Appeldoorn have created a wonderful guide that can be used in everyday life that allows adults, and the children and adolescents they love, to find the path back to their optimal state of mental health and well-being.

—Nimi Singh, MD, MPH, associate professor of Pediatrics, University of Minnesota

1. National Institute of Mental Health US Department of Health and Human Services, Mental Health in Adolescents, and NIH (2017). *See* https://www.hhs.gov/ash/oah/adolescent-development/mental-health/index.html.
2. America's Children and the Environment, Third Edition, Updated August 2017. Health/Neurodevelopmental Disorders. *See* https://www.epa.gov/sites/production/files/2017-07/documents/neurodevelopmental_updates_0.pdf.

INTRODUCTION

Why did we create *Moving Mountains*?

Because working with distressed children who struggle with ineffective coping strategies is hard! We have seen the deep pain of anger, helplessness, and turmoil in youth, and the very same emotions in adults when the interventions they try do not succeed. We have spent countless hours with families and practitioners doing our very best to recommend useful, logical strategies to help children self-regulate and succeed in their lives. However, we noticed over time that these same families and practitioners often returned to us frustrated and discouraged. The interventions that sounded so helpful and "common sense" in our offices or trainings only worked a small percentage of the time; and sometimes it depended on the day, or maybe even on what the child had for breakfast. Sometimes they did not actually work at all.

As we tried to understand this problem, we turned to the work of Dr. Bruce Perry, Dr. Daniel Siegel, Tina Payne Bryson, Jim and Lynea Gillen (*See Resources*), and others who express their concern that many parenting and classroom strategies, while helpful, do not take into consideration the neuroscience of emotional regulation of both parties in the equation: the child and the caregiver. Whether at school, home, or elsewhere, these clinicians (and we) believe that the caregiver-child relationship is the primary "engine" for all developmental change. This requires that children have enough of their "thinking brains" available to learn and implement the skills they need to self-regulate and become more resilient.

WHY DO WE CALL THIS AN *"INTEGRATIVE"* MANUAL?

The purpose of *Moving Mountains* is not necessarily to teach you a brand-new set of interventions, although we include a LOT of ideas in this manual! Rather, we are integrating information (including basic brain-based research), experience, and techniques to create a practical organizational framework.

This framework will help you determine when and how to use the interventions you'll learn as well as the ones you already know at different times and in different situations with children who are anxious and reactive.

We also focus on the most important tool you have: YOU.

In this manual, you'll have the opportunity to assess your own strengths, skills, and self-regulation patterns and how to best use them as tools for calming and centering youth.

HOW TO USE THIS MANUAL

> "Sometimes the most important thing in a whole day is the rest we take between two deep breaths."
> —Etty Hillesum

Our intention in creating this manual was not to have it sit on a shelf but to be used actively in our work with youth and families. So here are some ideas on how to begin:

INTRODUCTION

1 BECOME FAMILIAR
Become familiar with the Moving Mountains framework and each zone of activation

2 COMPLETE
Complete the section "What's in Your Backpack?" to assess your own nervous system's responses, needs, and triggers

3 SPECIFY THE CHILD
Complete the "What's in Your Backpack?" section with a particular child in mind

4 START USING IT
Start using the Moving Mountains framework as a way to organize and "file" strategies, tools, and techniques

What impact will reading and using this manual have on you and your work with children? We are hopeful that you will experience at least some of the positive changes that developing the Moving Mountains framework has brought to our practices, including:

- Improving your sense of effectiveness with some of the most difficult to manage behaviors and issues

- Creating new opportunities for healing, learning, and connection between us and the children/youth who need our help

- Having a new relationship with "self-care," a broad term which has come to mean anything enjoyable or healthy we do as a way to replenish ourselves. Understanding our own nervous systems, emotions, and sensory thresholds helps us create more targeted self-care. What we need to self-regulate and take care of ourselves can be very different day to day based on what experiences we have had, what zone we have escalated to, etc.

THE FOUNDATION

Because you are reading this manual, you probably already know one (or five, or twenty) anxious and reactive children very well. Let's take a moment though to more fully describe the children and adolescents who struggle with these issues.

Let's start with what we observe them doing, notice how we as adults tend to describe them, and work our way more deeply into the developmental pathways that cause them to struggle so much. Throughout this manual, we use three fictional young people to help illustrate how the Moving Mountains framework can be used to work with a wide range of issues and personalities.

THE FOUNDATION

MEET MICHAEL...

Michael is a ten-year-old boy in the fourth grade. He is usually receptive to directions and feedback from teachers. However, when he is very frustrated by work, classroom rules, or interactions with peers, Michael's behaviors escalate. His face flushes, his fists clench, he throws his paper and pencils down, and occasionally runs out of his classroom screaming things like, "I am OUT OF HERE! You all are SO STUPID!"

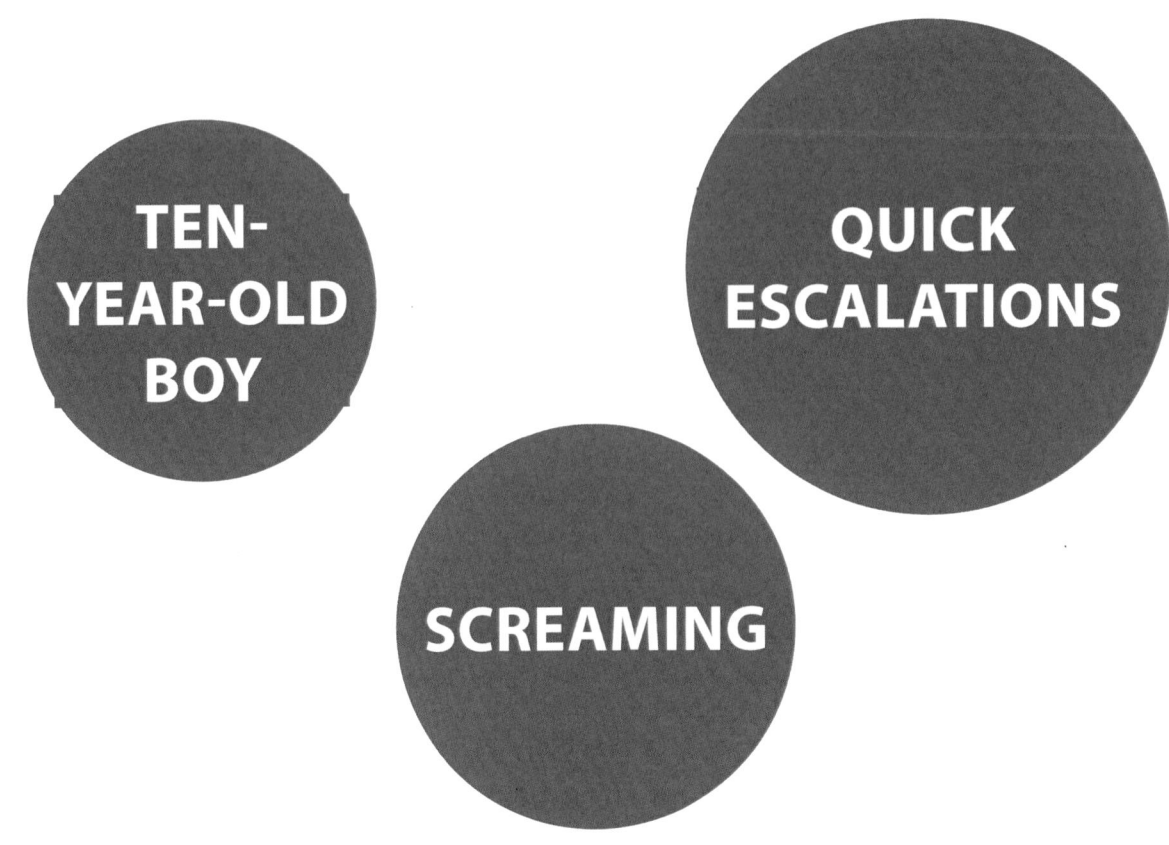

TEN-YEAR-OLD BOY

QUICK ESCALATIONS

SCREAMING

THE FOUNDATION

MEET SARAH...

Sarah is a seven-year-old girl in the first grade. Her mother and father describe her as "bossy," and when plans change or she doesn't get what she wants, she becomes loud and argumentative. She refuses to take a break and escalates if adults try to end conversations or walk away. Sarah is easily startled by noises and has many worries, including tornadoes, robbers, and being alone. At school, she spends time in the social worker's office several times a week when she is too upset to be in class. She has struggled with insomnia since being a preschooler, and her parents have had to develop an elaborate bedtime routine to help her fall asleep.

THE FOUNDATION

MEET TANYA...

Tanya is a fifteen-year-old girl in the 10th grade who is struggling with failing grades. Her parents report she gets plenty of sleep, but especially during stressful times during test-taking periods she frequently says "I'm tired" and seems lethargic or yells, "Leave me alone!" and appears panicky. Sometimes she puts her sweatshirt hood up and her head on her desk during class, and refuses to answer the teacher's requests to sit up.

FIFTEEN-YEAR-OLD GIRL

LETHARGIC

STRESS TEST TAKING

THE FOUNDATION

WHAT DO WE SEE?
Here is a list of characteristics and behaviors we observe in anxious, reactive youth:

INTENSITY

In our practice we call these "very VERY" young people, which means it is hard for them to find emotional middle ground. Whether they are happy, scared, angry, or sad, their feelings are big and often out of proportion to the situation at hand. Sometimes this also is accompanied by high levels of physical activity, or by needing to shut down and withdraw because their experiences are so overwhelming.

SENSITIVITY

Many of these young people have a "thin skin" when it comes to sensory experiences. They may be hugely affected by input such as light, sound, smells, or textures and may react dramatically when overstimulated.

RIGIDITY

In response to these overwhelming emotions, they often respond by attempting to control their environment. They may be labeled as "bossy" and "demanding," or they may react poorly in other ways to any changes in routine.

THE FOUNDATION

TANTRUMS VS MELTDOWNS

Not all explosions are created equal.

A tantrum is a behavioral outburst usually triggered by rigidity in a situation in which the child is attempting to force something to change (a limit or rule, a peer's decision, etc.).

A meltdown is different. As a result of feeling such enormous emotions and frustrations from too much sensory input, a child will lose coping strategies and overreact. Meltdowns are not voluntary and often consist of a fight/flight/freeze response.

Examples of meltdown behaviors include:

LASHING OUT

As a result of experiencing such enormous feelings, children sometimes go into a fight/flight/freeze response. Verbal aggression (swearing, yelling, screaming) and/or physical aggression toward people or objects (pushing, throwing, hitting, biting, etc.) are the "fight" part of this reaction.

RUNNING AWAY

Diving under tables, running out of the classroom or house, or tuning out and "disappearing" into books, video games, or other interests is the "flight" part of this reaction.

SHUTTING DOWN

When a child's system is totally overwhelmed, they are unable to fight or flee, and so they "freeze." This may look like spaciness, fatigue, blank looks, unresponsiveness, withdrawal, or quiet defiance.

THE FOUNDATION

WHAT DO WE SAY ABOUT THESE CHILDREN AND ADOLESCENTS?

Because we are human, the intensity of these reactions causes us (their helpers) to react as well. The following is a partial list of quotes from past Moving Mountains workshop participants describing what they or others say about these youth:

"They are out of control."

"Wow, they go zero to sixty in five seconds!"

"They can't listen to logic."

"They just refuse to use strategies."

"I tense up as soon as they get off the bus."

"When things get bad, it's like they are just gone . . . I can't reach them."

"I'm almost relieved when they don't come to session."

Intense emotions and behaviors in children almost inevitably cause strong reactions in adults. That is okay. Being honest with yourself about your thoughts, feelings, and responses to challenging young people is a really important part of trying to find ways to be an effective helper.

THE FOUNDATION

QUESTION: "NATURE? OR NURTURE?"
ANSWER: "YES!"

Now that we've talked about who these youth are, let's look at the "why" of their intensity, reactivity, and anxiety. In the same way that many roots of a tree can feed into the same branch, there are many developmental experiences which act as pathways for these issues to develop. This concept is called "developmental equifinality." (Cichetti and Rogosch, 1996)

For this chapter, we are dividing these pathways into two categories: External/Environmental and Internal/Organic. However, these two categories obviously influence and intertwine with each other.

ENVIRONMENTAL PATHWAYS

TRAUMA

Many who hear this word associate it with catastrophic events such as abuse, injury, or the loss of a loved one. However, in this manual, we define "trauma" as experiences that are overwhelming to a child's nervous system and trigger the flight/fight/freeze response. These events may not be readily recognized as traumatic when viewed from the outside. Unfortunately, the lives of many children and adolescents are full of these experiences.

FAMILY STRESSORS

These stressors could be within family relationships, such as marital conflict or the birth of a new sibling. They could also be stressors on the family system, such as economic struggle, a parent's job change, or a move.

SYSTEMIC COMMUNITY STRESS

Many children we work with are part of communities that are experiencing constant stress, prejudice, or marginalization. These include (but are not limited to) children of color, families living in poverty, LGBTQ youth, and immigrants/refugees.

GOODNESS-OF-FIT ISSUES

Sometimes parents and children simply have different personalities, sensory needs, and temperaments. For example, Marit's son needs to have loud music on to relax in the car, and she prefers silence and can become irritable with lots of noise. Goodness-of-fit issues are neither the child's fault nor the parent's fault, but they can cause stress on each of them.

THE FOUNDATION

Questions to consider

(*See* Worksheets section)

- What environmental stressors are the children you work with experiencing?

- What are the stressors in your community?

- How do these community stressors impact you personally?

INTERNAL/ORGANIC PATHWAYS

TEMPERAMENT

We are all born with certain innate characteristics and traits. Depending on what those are, a child's temperament can make it difficult for her or him to stay regulated in certain environments. And the same is true of adults. We look more at temperament in the chapter on self-assessment.

ATTENTION DEFICIT AND HYPERACTIVITY DISORDER (ADD/ADHD)

Young people who have ADD/ADHD struggle with executive function tasks, including difficulties with transitions, resisting change, low frustration tolerance, etc. It is easy to see how these problems could lead to explosiveness and rigidity.

ANXIETY

Anxiety causes the central nervous system to be "keyed up" to a high level of tension and activation. If children are anxious, their bodies are already close to being overwhelmed.

DEPRESSION

For children/youth experiencing depression, two things are often true. First, in the opposite phenomenon to anxiety, the central nervous system is in shut-down mode, causing collapse, lethargy, and fatigue. Second, depression often causes sadness in adults; but in children, it manifests more frequently as extreme irritability and loss of interest in activities (including schoolwork).

THE FOUNDATION

SENSORY PROCESSING ISSUES

We need sensory information to function, and we get that input through our five senses (sight, sound, touch, smell, and taste). We also receive constant input through the other senses: proprioception (the sense of where our body stops and the world starts) and vestibular (knowing where our bodies are in space). When all goes well, we are able to integrate and deal with the information from all these sensory channels without any problem. But issues arise if we have difficulty doing that and are sensitive to certain kinds of input.

Imagine being at a crowded county fair. It is the hottest day of the summer, you are jostling elbows with huge crowds of people, the air is full of the smells of people, food, and livestock. You are a little queasy from the rollercoaster you just went on, and your ears are full of the sounds of the carnival barkers and ride music. This can be what life is like every day for a child with sensory-processing concerns, which can lead to reactivity, rigidity, and avoidance of anything that feels "too much."

AUTISM SPECTRUM DISORDER

Children and youth with ASD represent an enormous continuum encompassing a huge diversity of needs. However, what most of them have in common is a combination of sensory issues and nervous systems that are highly reactive to any changes in their environment or routines. They may also have difficulty reading social and emotional cues.

Questions to consider

(*See* Worksheets section)

- What are the common internal/organic issues or diagnoses you observe in the children and youth you are working with?

- How do these issues impact your relationship with these children?

- What internal/organic issues or diagnoses do you yourself struggle with?

IMPACT AND OUTCOMES

When we think of areas of impact within the child, the adult, and the relationship, we want to address the three domains constantly: **cognitive, physical, and emotional.** These three domains are intrinsically connected and affect each other.

> "We are not just heads, we are heads with bodies attached."
>
> —Gisela S. De Domenico (*See* glossary)

How we think affects how we show up physically and emotionally.

How we show up physically affects how we think and feel.

THE FOUNDATION

AREAS OF IMPACT WITHIN THE *CHILD*

COGNITIVELY
- Shut down
- Rigidity
- Negative self-talk

PHYSICALLY
- Sleep disruption
- Elimination issues
- Headaches
- Stomachaches
- Low energy
- Fight/flight/freeze

EMOTIONALLY
- Difficulty with friendships/fighting
- Withdrawn
- Overwhelmed
- Confused
- Quitting activities
- Stuck on one emotion
- Arguing
- Swearing
- Screaming

AREAS OF IMPACT WITHIN THE *ADULT*

COGNITIVELY
- Shutting down
- Dismissive, cold, or angry language
- Incessant talking/lecturing
- Negativity
- Controlling behavior

PHYSICALLY
- Sleep disruption
- Elimination issues
- Headaches
- Stomachaches
- Body aches
- Overall exhaustion

EMOTIONALLY
- Irritability
- Short temperedness
- Withdrawal
- Quitting activities/shutting down
- Remaining stuck in one emotion
- Feeling incompetent/ineffective
- Arguing
- Swearing
- Screaming
- Sadness
- Confusion
- Burnout

THE FOUNDATION

AREAS OF IMPACT ON THE *ADULT-CHILD RELATIONSHIP*

Relationships with "attuned" adults are the most important tools children and young people have as they navigate their lives. When we look at the effects of emotional reactivity on children and adults, it is no surprise that these relationships can become seriously impaired.

How does this happen?

COGNITIVELY
- Decreased ability to negotiate
- Decreased problem-solving skills
- Angry, dismissive language toward one another

PHYSICALLY
- Awareness of each other's tense body language
- Reactivity and anger causing the adult and child to be triggered by each other and go back and forth in a "mutual" tantrum
- Exhaustion

EMOTIONALLY
- Loss of positive regard for each other
- Loss of the ability to empathize and partner with each other as a "team"
- Sadness and confusion

WHAT NEEDS TO HAPPEN FIRST?

While adults and children/youth are each affected physically, emotionally, and mentally by these issues and behaviors, the adult needs to be the one who first steps back and finds a way to regroup. We call this getting to our upstairs brain faster than the children (See Resources). Too often we adults find ourselves instantly matching the child's level of intensity with our own, leading to even higher levels of escalation. To avoid intense engagement, one of the most powerful interventions we can do is to step back. The chapter, "What's in Your Backpack?" is designed to help you assess your own sensory thresholds, which can provide insight and strategies on how to keep yourself regulated in times of stress.

Triggered

Exhausted, confused, out of comfort zone

Lost ability to empathize and partner with young person

THE MOUNTAIN

A framework to understand what's happening

As noted in the Introduction, we have known hundreds of families, teachers, and other adults who have children with intensity and reactivity—all of whom have worked very hard to learn effective strategies to help them. And we are lucky to live in a time when we can reap the benefits of more research on childrens' emotions and behaviors than ever before. People can read from the research, consult experts, take classes and webinars, go to conferences, and much, much more. Unfortunately, over and over again we have found ourselves counseling frustrated grownups (and youth) who are upset because the interventions they learned, while excellent, were not working consistently.

As Sarah's mother put it, "Everything I read says that breathing is the key to calming down. Yesterday she was freaking out about practicing flute, and I told her to take a deep breath. And she screamed and threw the flute at my head! So was I doing it wrong? Or is nothing ever going to work?" As she spoke, Sarah hung her head and her cheeks turned bright red in embarrassment. Like so many families, both she and her mother were feeling defeated and hopeless.

The Moving Mountains framework was developed to show families, teachers, and practitioners that the issue is not only what to do to help a child that is reactive or anxious, but when to do it, depending on:

1. How activated and upset that child is and, as a consequence,

2. How much of the child's brain is still "switched on" and available for use.

THE MOUNTAIN

The concept of how increasing stress changes and activates different parts of the brain is certainly not a new one. We encourage you to explore some of the important work listed in the Resources section at the end of this book, particularly that of Bruce Perry, Daniel Siegel (and Tina Payne Bryson), Anne Gearity, and also Leah Kuypers, author of the Zones of Regulation curriculum implemented in schools and therapeutic settings.

The Moving Mountains framework provides a way for adults to become more intentional about what they do and how they behave with children in distress. One way to look at it: Moving Mountains integrates these ideas about stress and the brain into a "filing" system to help you make choices about how and when to use the interventions to best help youth when they are anxious and overwhelmed.

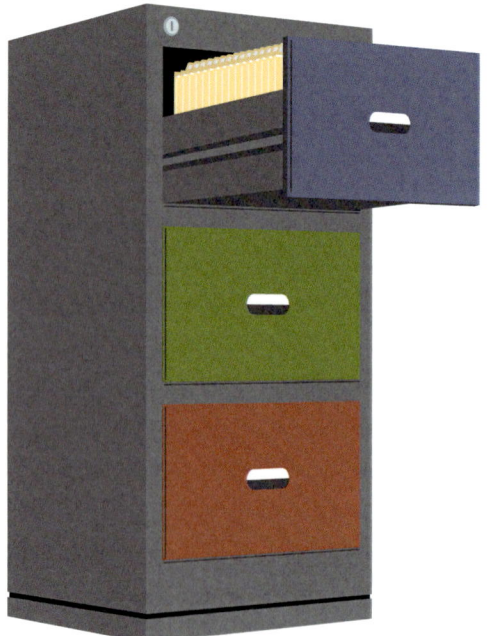

We are well aware of the irony that two people from the flat Midwest would come up with the metaphor of a mountain, but we invite you to imagine a "mountain" of stress and activation.

THE FOOTHILLS

The Foothills are the lowest part of a mountain and in some ways are no different than being on flat ground. The air quality is good and there is often a variety of trees, wildflowers, and grasses. In the Foothills it's possible to build gentle climbing paths and many people can easily build houses for themselves.

THE TREELINE

The Treeline is the highest point on a mountain at which trees can grow. The earth is often rockier, more difficult to navigate, and vegetation is sparse. The air has begun to thin, although climbers don't need extra oxygen.

THE SNOWLINE

The Snowline is exactly what it sounds like: the area extending up to the mountain summit which has thin air and is covered in nothing but rocks, snow, and ice.

As we explore in the next sections, human bodies and minds are like mountains in this way. When we are calm or just a little upset, we have all of our coping skills, resilience, and abilities (our own "vegetation") available to us (the Foothills). As we become more upset, those skills begin to turn off, and we shift more and more into the survival mode of a Fight/flight/freeze response (the Treeline). You'll notice the word "we," because this process is not just true for young people—it is true for all human beings regardless of age. We are all capable of going into our own personal "Snowline" of Fight/flight/freeze. However, for most of us, it takes something intensely stressful to get us there (a loved one being in imminent danger, being attacked, a car accident, etc.). And for the youth we work with, it can take very little (the scrape of a chair, a perceived criticism, a change in routine, receiving a text).

We know this is much easier than it sounds! At the end of each section of our framework, you will see a paragraph called, "What Are the Adults Doing?" where we include suggestions on how adults can remain calm and centered in our bodies so our whole brain is available while a child is agitated and melting down.

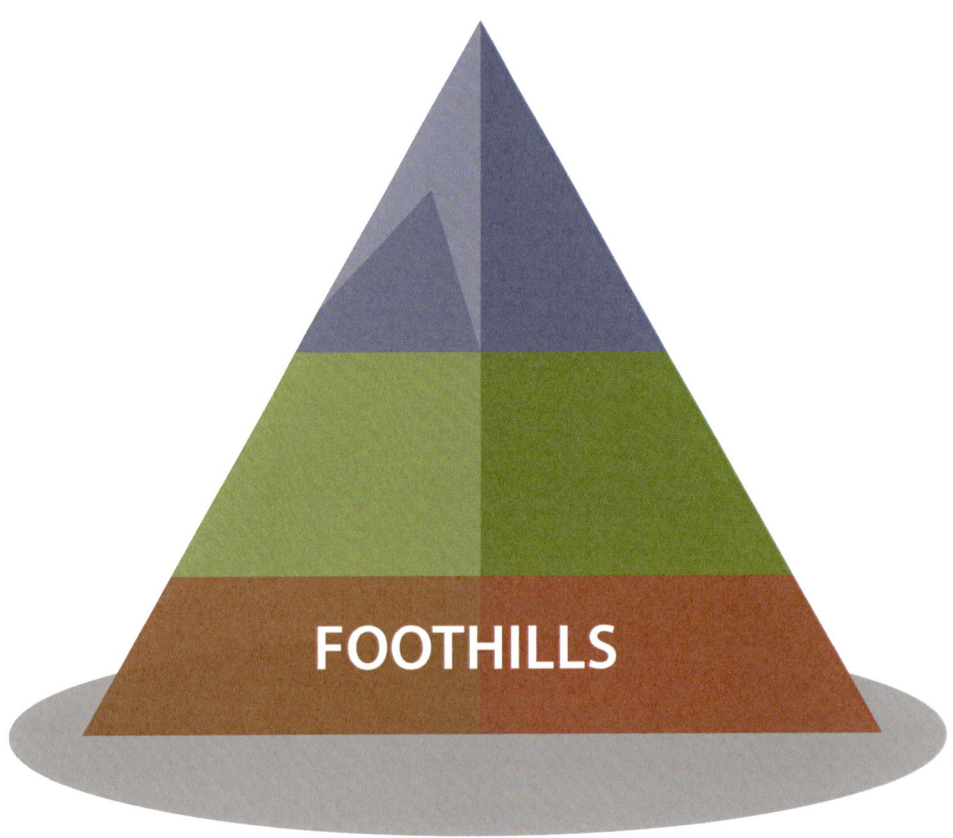

COGNITIVELY

All areas of the brain are available, including our ability to learn new skills to help use logic and problem solve.

PHYSICALLY

We see mild arousal such as tapping pencil, legs moving, getting up out of chair. Outward signs of mild sympathetic arousal.

EMOTIONALLY

We may start to see changes in mood and behavior, mild irritability and frustration, but able to self-regulate with some support.

THE FOOTHILLS

CASE STUDY: MICHAEL

It is right after lunchtime, and Michael's fourth-grade classroom is buzzing with activity. His teacher has just introduced a new reading concept and handed out worksheets. The children are talking and giggling as they settle in to work. Michael puts his hands over his ears as he reads his worksheet, and tells his neighbor to "STOP TALKING!"

The teacher quiets the classroom. Michael continues working but appears somewhat frustrated, looking at the teacher with wide eyes. The teacher approaches him, and says, "Michael, I get it—this is stressing you out. It was really loud in here, wasn't it?" Michael nods. The teacher then says to the class, "Okay, everyone, pencils down. Everyone stand up behind their chairs so I can show you how to do a Chair Dog stretch." All the children, including Michael, stand up. Following the teacher's instructions, they place their hands on the backs of their chairs and stretch out their bodies, taking three slow breaths.

The teacher praises her students and says, "Okay, I think we're going to start doing this every day after lunch." After the children sit down and start working again, she quietly talks to Michael, explaining to him that this kind of stretch "helps the stress get out of our bodies." He nods in understanding.

DESCRIPTION

As explained in the previous section, in the foothills of an actual mountain, the elevation is slightly higher, but the air is full of oxygen, and wildlife and vegetation are available and plentiful. In the Moving Mountains framework, the "Foothills" are a "zone" of mild frustration and activation. Children may be frustrated or anxious, but because they are still in the Foothills, all or most of their brains are still available to them to use. They can problem-solve, they can incorporate verbal feedback, and they can respond to adult suggestions. As youth become more dysregulated and are at higher "zones" of activation, their amygdalae begin to shut down these cognitive areas of the brain (e.g., the prefrontal cortex).

IN THE FOOTHILLS

His teacher notices that even though Michael is upset, he is able to take in what she is telling him and can see her perspective.

Teacher: "Michael, I get it—this is really frustrating. Can you think of something else to do with that chair? In fact, let me show you a stretch called Chair Dog. Step back a little bit, put your hands on the chair and stretch your body back [demonstrates]. It might help get that frustration out. Let's do it together and take three slow breaths."

Michael grumbles but follows her instructions and takes three slow breaths, then sits down again and, after a minute, he pulls out a sheet of paper and starts his assignment.

NOT IN THE FOOTHILLS

While she is talking to him about the assignment, the teacher doesn't notice that Michael does not seem to be registering what she saying. In fact, he is becoming more insistent that he should not be doing his work and bangs the chair on the floor even more emphatically.

Teacher: "Michael, I get it. Can you think of something else to do with that chair?" [Michael picks the chair up, whirls around and throws it as hard as he can at the child behind him.] Michael has now moved to Snowline.

Because of this, the Foothills is the only zone in which we can ask kids to use logic, problem-solving, and empathy. In fact, it is imperative that children learn and experience a wide variety of strategies when they are in the Foothills. They can then put them in their metaphorical "backpack" and pull them out to use when they are farther up the mountain.

STRATEGIES THAT WORK

CALMING

When we use the word "calming," we are speaking about inhibiting movement, quieting, and slowing down the pace. This approach is much more effective in the Foothills of mild upset than when children have moved up the mountain to a higher zone. No truly agitated person wants to be reminded to breathe or told to "just calm down!"

CURIOSITY AND SELF-MONITORING

The Foothills is also where we spend time noticing what interventions feel good to a child and helping her/him/they be aware of this as well. We might ask, "Do you like what I just showed you?" or, "How does that feel to you—what do you think?"

Once activities and skills are learned, we might ask a child to choose which ones they want to do with us. Becoming curious about what helps them regulate is not only calming but helps a child feel empowered and able to ask for and receive help.

In Foothills, youth have more of their brains available than in any other zone, meaning that their amygdalae have not yet begun to shut off logical thinking, empathy, and/or a willingness and ability to learn new information.

Because of this, the Foothills are the only zone in which we teach children new self-regulation strategies. We often recommend that these strategies, such as breathwork, mindful movement, etc., be practiced on a regular basis as opposed to when problems arise, much like a daily "sensory diet" in occupational therapy.

THE FOOTHILLS

INTERVENTIONS: CALMING TOOLS

Prone belly breathing

Often when we are able to lie belly down, we are able to feel more connected and grounded. We are also able to access diaphragmatic/belly breathing more easily as we receive input from the ground and can feel the belly expand and contract. If it is comfortable, press your forehead into your hands, one palm up, releasing the eyes and eyebrows. Begin slow, deep belly breathing.

Words you might use to guide a child/youth: Lie on the floor, belly down. Begin to breathe slowly in and out so you can feel the belly rise and fall like waves of the ocean. Try to have your breath move slowly in and out as you feel the belly puff into the floor. Added bonus: make a pillow with your hands, and allow your forehead to rest on your hands, gently pressing into the space between the eyebrows. Maybe say to yourself, "soft eyes."

Child's pose

This exercise allows youth to reduce sensory input and slow down their heart rate. It is an inversion where the head goes below the heart and starts to lower blood pressure and heart rate, and will often give the body a sense of safety. Place big toes together and allow the knees to widen and arms stretch out to the side, or hands stack, letting the head and neck rest.

Down dog

Down dog is a movement that gives the body deep proprioceptive input which can give us a sense of safety. It is also an inversion which means the head goes below the heart, creating a relaxation response to bring fresh blood into the brain and lower heart rate and blood pressure.

Come on to all fours with hands under shoulders and knees under and slightly behind hips. Point your fingers straight ahead and spread them like rays of the sun. Press down through the four corners of the hands and feet. Activate and straighten the arms. Turn the toes under, and press thighs and hips toward the wall behind you, creating an upside down "V."

Keep your arms straight with head and chest slightly lifted up to create a flat back from head to hips. If the backs of your legs are tight, bend your knees slightly and lift your tail up to the sky. Stay here for three to five breaths. Then look at your hands and walk your feet to your hands, coming into a forward fold. Place hands on your hips, draw your elbows back, and then slowly inhale your body up.

Legs up the wall

Sit sideways against a wall. Then swing legs up the wall and allow your shoulders and head to lightly touch the floor. Allow your sternum bone to lift and your chin to move slightly away from the chest. Legs can be up the wall 3–15 minutes. If your legs get tired you can bend your knees and put your feet flat on the wall or place the soles of your feet together. To come down, slowly lower the legs and then allow your body to roll over to one side. Make a pillow with your arm and rest your head and draw your knees in, resting here in fetal position Then slowly use the strength of your hands and arms to lift you up into a seated position.

Comfort self-soothing

Aromas/Aromatherapy: Aromas are a powerful and "efficient" tool to activate and calm the nervous system. If you are interested, we encourage you to read any of the excellent books or other sources published on the uses of aromatherapy. As a cautionary note: not all children (or adults) respond to a particular scent the same way, so we discourage spraying aromas into the air unless all the people in that room have agreed to it. It's often helpful to have a range of calming scents available (e.g., lavender, citrus, spearmint, vanilla) to provide children with choices, depending on their preference. Essential oils and blends often come in rollerball or "inhaler" tubes, or you can put a drop or two on a cotton ball for a child to carry with them.

Textures

Touch is one of our primary senses, and having objects with soothing textures accessible to children in our work environment can be very calming. Examples include soft throw blankets, "taggie" blankets to fidget with (even for older children), squishy soft pillows, etc. These can be placed in the corner of a classroom, in a child's room at home, etc.

Slow pace

Reading: For children and teens who enjoy books or graphic novels, a twenty to thirty-minute reading break can provide the opportunity to keep recovering from a stressful situation by entering into a whole new world and storyline! This distraction can provide the nervous system a much-needed "reset." We like to have a range of books with "therapeutic" topics like stress management available, but it's also important to allow children to read their own preferred materials.

Puzzles: Working on puzzles can be another way to recover from a stressful situation. Puzzles take concentration and maybe just the right kind of distraction needed to calm the body.

Pick-Up Sticks: a classic game that can be purchased online or in stores. The rules of the game can be flexible, but generally speaking it's played by dumping the brightly colored sticks into a pile on the floor and taking turns attempting to ease them out of the pile and pick them up one at a time—without moving any of the others! In addition to being a blast, this game encourages children to slow their movements, focus their energy and attention, and quiet down.

WHAT ARE THE ADULTS DOING *DURING* THE INTERVENTION?

- Drop "energy"/ground feet. Bring all your attention down to your feet. Allow your toes to spread, and press the pads of your feet into the earth. Take a few breaths, and perhaps say to yourself, "I am here," or "I am grounded," or "I have got this."

- Breathe slowly. Allow the exhales to be twice as long as your inhale. For example, inhale for two counts, and exhale for four counts.

- Lower your tone and voice level.

- When in the Foothills, music and rhythms can be very soothing and can activate the vagus nerve. Together with a young person, drum out the beat of a song they like using your hands on a table or your lap. Encourage them to sing, hum, or rap along. For younger children, rhythmic clapping games or special elaborate handshakes can be both regulating and a way to connect with you or with peers.

- When we are calm or just a little upset, we have all of our coping skills, resilience, and abilities (our own "vegetation") available to us. As we become more upset, those begin to turn off, and we shift more and more into the survival mode of a fight/flight/freeze response. You'll notice the word "we" again, because this process is not just true for children/youth—it is true for all human beings regardless of age. We are all capable of going into our own personal "Snowline" of fight/flight/freeze, and it is important to work on our own regulation to help regulate the children we're trying to help.

WHAT ARE THE ADULTS DOING *AFTER* THE INTERVENTION?

Staying regulated throughout the day is challenging. However, if we can be proactive and think about what helps us feel more regulated/connected and then use those strategies, we can return to center and bounce back more easily. Ideas might be: walk it off, inversion, interlace arms behind your back and open shoulders and chest, use an essential oil, etc.

THE FOOTHILLS

TOOLS FOR SELF-MONITORING

Scaling 1–10

One way to encourage self-monitoring is to help children find ways to rate or "score" their feelings.

Examples of scaling include:

- Verbally put feelings on a scale of 1 to 10, with 1 being totally calm, and 10 being "the biggest anger ever."

- Use a picture (which youth can point to) of the Zones of Regulation (*See* Resources) of "blue/green/yellow/red."

- Create language: Another way to encourage children to self-monitor is to help them decide what they want to call the intense emotions they feel. Grownup words like "anxiety" or "activation" might not mean a lot to a child, but they will be able to tell you about their "stress" or their "big mad" or their "this is too much" feelings.

THE FOOTHILLS

Pulse count

Taking our pulse is a really simple way to get into the body and receive immediate feedback on what is happening inside. Place fingers under the jaw bone to find the groove in your neck. Gently press to feel the heartbeat. Take a fifteen-second pulse count and multiply by four. If the heart is beating really fast, and you are not working out, start to slow down your breathing so you can notice spaces between the beats.

Breathing with the Hoberman Sphere*

Daily Practice Script: "John, how many breaths do you think the group needs between five and eight? Let's breathe together six times. Breathe in (Hoberman expands), breathe out (Hoberman closes), five more times. Then sit for fifteen seconds, and notice how the mind and body feels. How does the room feel?"

Tracing your hand

Breathe in and trace up the thumb, breathe out tracing down the thumb, breathe in, trace up the index finger, breathe out, tracing down the finger. Continue to trace the entire hand while you are slowly breathing in and out.

Hands on heart and belly

Breathe in from the belly into the heart and then in from heart into belly. Breathe slowly five to twelve times.

*Yoga Calm© Activity used with permission, yogacalm.org

Moving Mountains Manual   31

FOOTHILLS APPLICATION

These worksheets can be used as a tool to record your observations about behaviors and list possible interventions in the Foothills. Below, the sheets are filled out as if we were Michael's teacher (or other school staff). The Appendix section of this manual contains reproducible application worksheets for you to copy and use in your work with the youth you know.

OBSERVED BEHAVIORS

Puts his hands over his ears

Yelling at his classmate/desk neighbor during work time

Sometimes yells at the teacher or the whole class

Frustrated—goes from zero to 60 quickly

Gets flushed in the face, fists clench

Sometimes runs out of the room

Does seem to calm down fairly quickly

POSSIBLE TRIGGERS/CIRCUMSTANCES

Seems to happen at work time—classroom gets really loud with talking—is noise a trigger?

Also happens when he is frustrated with rules and when things don't go the way he expected

INTERVENTIONS

Hand Tracing Breathing (page 31)—teach to the class and practice daily

Hands on Heart and Belly (page 31)—teach to the class and practice once or twice a week

Design a corner in the room where Michael can take a break

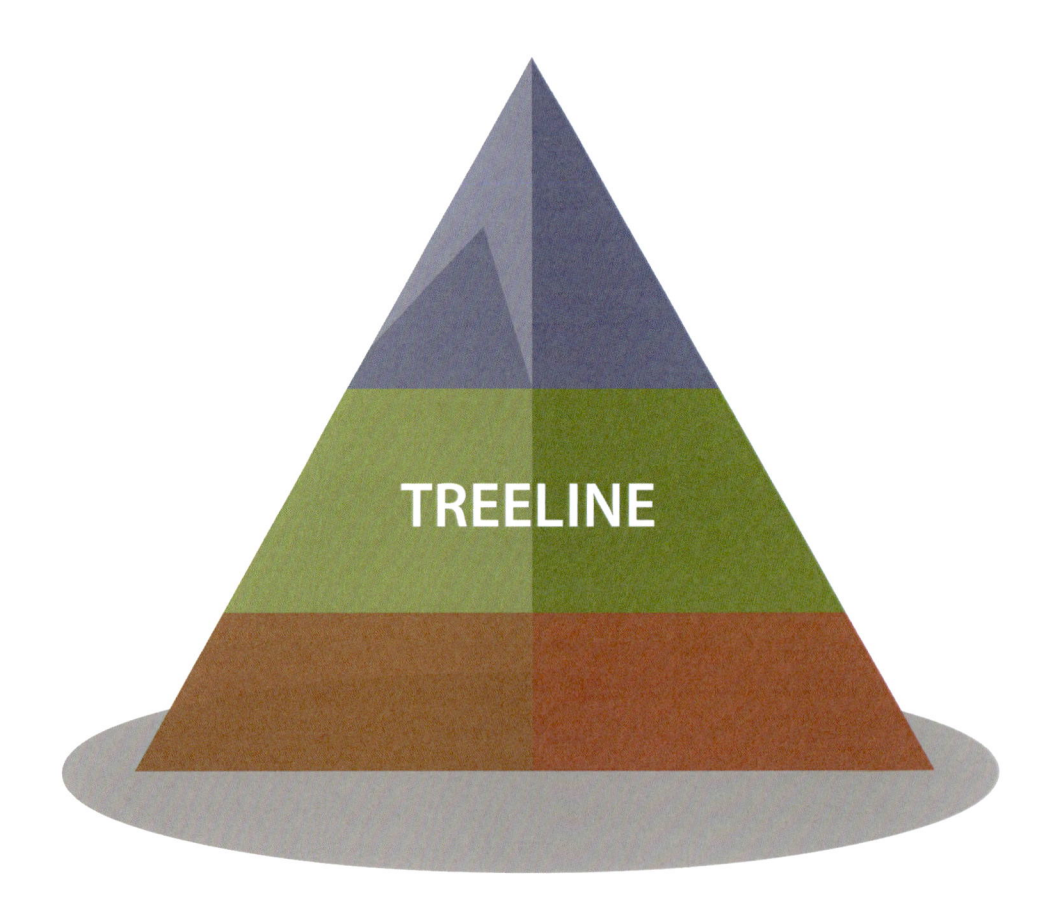

COGNITIVELY

Ability to process is unpredictable. When it comes to logical thought, "lights are flickering on and off."

PHYSICALLY

Evidence of moderate arousal, irritable outbursts, being "hyper," and restless movement.

EMOTIONALLY

Reactive, increased push back toward others or withdrawal.

THE TREELINE

CASE STUDY: SARAH

It is a summer Saturday evening and seven-year-old Sarah has spent a long day with her family at the lake swimming and then out to eat at a noisy, crowded restaurant. The family is finally returning home close to bedtime. Sarah's mother, Julie, tells her to put on her pajamas and brush her teeth. Although Sarah eventually complies, she immediately begins loudly arguing about every step in the bedtime routine process—what pajamas she wants to wear, what cup she wants for her bedtime water, etc.

Sarah stalls getting into bed, becoming more hyperactive and running repeatedly into the living room to look out the window. Her mother asks what Sarah is looking at, and she replies in a loud, tense voice, "I just need to check to see if there's a tornado coming. I thought I saw lightning." Julie points to the clear evening sky and says, "See? It's okay, there's no storm."

NOT YET IN THE TREELINE

Sarah looks at the clear sky and says, "Yeah, but I still think there might be a storm . . . could one come all of a sudden?" Sarah's father pulls up a weather app and shows her the completely clear radar forecast for the area, and she says, "Okay."

Julie cuddles Sarah and reminds her, "Your dad and I will always keep you safe, no matter the weather, and we have a plan for that." Sarah agrees to go to bed and listens to a story before falling asleep.

(Because Sarah can respond to logic-based, problem-solving interventions, she is in Foothills.)

THE TREELINE

IN THE TREELINE

After Julie points at the sky, Sarah's face becomes flushed, and she continues to ask multiple questions about the weather as she zooms around the living room and jumps on the couch, and is not reassured by her father offering to show her the weather radar. Julie walks over to Sarah and says calmly, "Okay, it's time to chop up some of that tornado worry and blow it away—like we've been practicing." With her mother's help, Sarah does Conductor Breath (See page 44) three times, and then moves into a standing Forward Fold. Julie keeps talking to a minimum but reminds Sarah what comes next, which is to curl on the floor in Child's Pose. Julie places her hands on Sarah's back and has her breathe in and out very slowly, and proceeds to tell her a soothing story highlighting a few fun things of the day. Sarah rolls over and reaches up for a hug, saying, "We are so good at chopping up tornado worry!" Julie smiles and agrees, and helps Sarah settle in her room for bed.
(Because Sarah can't respond to verbal, logic-based interventions but can respond to body-based interventions she has learned before, she is in Treeline.)

DESCRIPTION

On a real mountain, as we ascend in height, the landscape starts to change. The vegetation that was so thick and lush in the foothills thins out, and the soil becomes rockier and less able to support life. The Treeline is what we call the highest elevation at which trees and other plant life can grow.

Similarly, as a child begins to escalate up the "mountain" of agitation, things get rockier, and they are less able to "grow" logical strategies or the ability to stay emotionally connected to us. We begin to see changes in mood, body, and behavior as her/his amygdala starts to take over and shut down the "thinking brain." This can be a real challenge for adults trying to respond. The child can be coherent one minute, and then the next minute not be responsive. She can be talking to (or at) us, but may not take in anything we're saying or will misinterpret and be reactive to even the most benign questions. Other changes are more physiological, and you may notice one or more of the following signs of increased tension and stress:

- Flushed face

- Faster breathing

- Higher, tighter, and louder voice

- Muscle tension (shoulders going up, clenching jaw, hands curling into fists)

INTERVENTIONS

Imagine something very aggravating happening to you in your day-to-day life. Perhaps a boss gave you a totally unfair and/or negative review, or you got rear-ended by a careless driver, or someone you thought was your friend took something you said out of context and started spreading a false rumor about you. Think about how stressed or even angry you might feel at being treated this way!

Now imagine what would happen if a well-meaning person said to you, "Forget about how you feel. You just need to calm down and take a deep breath."

When we do this visualization at our workshops, we usually hear a big wave of laughter and people call out things like, "No WAY!" "That is NOT helpful" or even "That person better get out of my way!"

Children escalating into the Treeline zone have tense bodies and minds flooding with cortisol and adrenaline. Asking them to "Just calm down" will not be helpful or effective! In the Treeline zone, we focus instead on ***discharging stress through connecting, mobilizing, and releasing strategies.*** This helps bring the nervous system back into the Foothills zone where language and logic can be used.

STRATEGIES THAT WORK

CONNECT

When a child is becoming agitated, our first impulse as adults is often to immediately "clamp down" and direct or discipline their behavior. However, even though this may seem counterintuitive, emotionally "joining" or connecting with a child can be most effective way to begin. According to Daniel Siegel and Tina Payne Bryson, emotional connection serves the purpose of moving a child from reactivity to receptivity (See Resources). We connect by being physically, emotionally, and mentally present to one another. Connection can be verbal, for example, "I am here for you," "This is frustrating," "I am sorry this happened." In non-verbal connection, the adult's breathing slows down, the face is relaxed, feet are connected to the earth to show I am here for you. It is critical that our words and our body match.

MOBILIZE

This is preparation to do something. Within the body is a sense of wanting to move or get away. One of our favorite effective activities include fight games, such as sword fighting. We have often been asked if sword fighting contributes or reinforces violent acting-out behavior. However, from a child's body perspective, this is a body that needs to mobilize, push against; and the body will do this in an "appropriate" or "not appropriate" way. Finding ways for the body to mobilize in an appropriate way is preferred.

RELEASE

Releasing is about setting "free," letting go, moving through. Interventions that allow that body to dissipate the energy are most helpful. Physical movement that includes powerful exhales help move the "large emotions" through. (See description of Conductor Breath on page 44).

TOOLS FOR CONNECTING, MOBILIZING, AND RELEASING

Back to back breathing

Sit back to back on the floor, and begin to slow down your breathing. If you want, close your eyes and start connecting to each other's breath. You may notice heat on your back. If you would like, bring attention to your heart and start breathing from your heart to your partner's heart. Stay here until you feel both bodies begin to calm.

Back breathing

Have child get into child's pose and, with permission, place your hands on the child's lower back. Have the child begin to to breathe into your hands, eliciting a diaphragmatic breathing pattern.*

*Yoga Calm© Activity used with permission, yogacalm.org

THE TREELINE

CONNECT

Point-of-view pie chart

This activity works best on a white board, but really all you need is a piece of paper and something to write with. The adult draws a circle and then says to the upset child something along the lines of, "Okay . . . I see you are really upset. I'm going to make a pie chart of what I think you might be thinking and feeling. But I'm probably going to get it wrong, so you'll have to correct me."

The adult then makes a pie chart with each "slice" representing the size of a worry, thought, or feeling. This gives the message that the adult is genuinely interested in the child, sees the child as having many complex thoughts and feelings, AND the child usually takes great delight in erasing and correcting the pie chart to make it accurate!

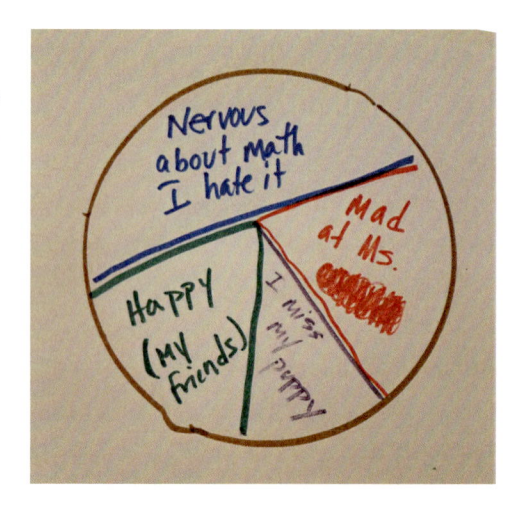

Mirroring/matching

As Daniel Siegel and Tina Payne Bryson write in *No Drama Discipline* (*see* Resources), before redirecting a child we need to connect with them. Sometimes, a powerful way to help a child descend from Treeline back into Foothills is simply to let them know you really, really understand how upset they are.

Mirroring/matching takes the "but" out of what we are doing. For example, Instead of saying, "I know you are really angry, but you HAVE to get out of the hallway," an adult working to mirror might say, "I know you are really, really angry. Wow, I can see how upset you are. I want to help figure this out."

MOBILIZE

ACTIVITIES

In order for youth to access an intervention, they must have learned and practiced skills in a calm state. Therefore all activities are taught in the Foothills. Then when the body is in an agitated state, one can access the skill.

Un-freeze movement

In this variation of freeze tag, it is helpful to have a drum, and beat the drum while children walk around the room. After (amount of time) stop the drum and have them freeze, then beat the drum again and have them walk, then freeze again. This activity is helpful as it allows the body to experience what it means to freeze and then get out of the freeze state. This felt sense of agency can be very powerful.*

Rolling, twisting, inversions

The yoga movement of rolling back and forth and side to side on your back, twisting (see photo on page 43) and inverting (bringing the head below the heart) allows the body to "move/mobilize." The inversions (see photo on page 27) give input into the vestibular and proprioceptive systems in the body, helping the body move to homeostasis.

Self-hug

This sounds simple, yet it is one of the most quick and powerful interventions, as it gives direct input into the body by providing deep touch pressure, which is not only soothing but can be organizing.

Playing catch

Tossing or rolling a ball back and forth is actually a connecting and mobilizing intervention. Simple as it sounds, it provides the adult and child with a playful way to engage with each other while also giving the body an easy opportunity to move and discharge tension.

*Yoga Calm© Activity used with permission, yogacalm.org

THE TREELINE

RELEASE

Releasing is about letting go, setting "free," moving through. Interventions that allow the body to dissipate excess energy are very helpful, and the key to this release is the ventral vagal response. The vagus nerve is a powerful part of the autonomic nervous system responsible for regulation. When the ventral vagal pathway is activated, our heart rate and breathing become slower and more rhythmic. More importantly, we are able to use relationships and social engagement to help us deal with stress and negative emotions. As the author Deb Dana says, "it's where we can acknowledge distress and explore options, reach out for support, and develop organized responses." (See Resources). This is exactly the state of being we want to get to in children, youth, and adults, and most of the activities in this manual are designed with that in mind.

Here are some additional strategies which directly "hack" the vagus nerve, meaning that they work quickly to activate a ventral vagal response. These activities should ideally be taught when children are in Foothills and then practiced with the help of adults when they are in Treeline.

- Humming or singing (either alone or with others)
- Drinking cold water
- Splashing cool/cold water on the face, ideally from the chin upwards (Dion, see Resources)
- Pressing gently but firmly on the top of the head with both hands
- Breathing with long, slow exhales which are longer than inhales

TOOLS FOR RELEASING

Forward bends/back bends

These can be super helpful in regulating a body. Forward bends are inversions and tend to allow the body to calm and "cool" down, lowering heart rate and blood pressure. Back bends tend to allow the body to energize and become more alert.

Shaking

This is a great way to release stress in the body. One way to teach this is to have the youth keep their feet connected in one place on the floor, and allow the rest of the upper body to shake. Try all directions, high, low, side to side. As you are shaking, sometimes it is helpful to think about what you want to "shake off." Put your favorite song on and try shaking for two to five minutes.

Movements

Conductor Breath, Forward Bend, Hip Flexor Release, and Twist are often active enough for more "agitated energy."

THE TREELINE

Breath work

In the Treeline zone, the body is often in a more agitated state, so it is important to meet the body where it is.

- The Conductor Breath is a releasing breath exercise that allows the body to release with a powerful exhale. This is an important breathing exercise to teach as a preventive tool so that, when children are upset, they have strategies to use to reduce anxiety and tension. Stand with feet at least hip-width apart, bend your knees slightly. Inhale and bring arms over your head; on your exhale, sweep the arms out to the side. Next inhale, bring the arms back overhead; and on the exhale, bend the knees and sweep the arms down and back with knees slightly bent. Repeat three times. The last two times, let go of something that is frustrating or getting in the way of you being your best self. If it feels okay, move into forward bend for three to five breaths.

- *Check the child's zone—can calming tools from the Foothills be used?*

WHAT ARE THE ADULTS DOING *DURING* THE INTERVENTION?

- Once again drop "energy"/ground feet. Bring all your attention down to your feet. Allow your toes to spread, and press the pads of your feet to the earth. Allow your energy to drop toward your feet. Take a few breaths into the feet and perhaps say to yourself, "I am here" or "I am grounded" or "I've got this."
- Take some slow breaths focusing more on the exhale.
- Lower your tone and voice level, and keep words to a minimum.

WHAT ARE THE ADULTS DOING *AFTER* THE INTERVENTION?

Just as in Foothills, if we can be proactive and think about what helps us feel more regulated and connected and then use those strategies, we can return to center and bounce back more easily. Ideas to try: walk it off, forward bend, interlace arms behind your back and fold forward, getting a chest expansion.

"I AM HERE."
"I AM GROUNDED."
"I'VE GOT THIS."

TREELINE APPLICATION

These worksheets can be used as a tool to record your observations about behaviors and list possible interventions in the Treeline. As an example, the sheets below are filled out as if we were Sarah's parents. The Appendix section of this manual contains reproducible application worksheets for you to copy and use in your work with the youth you know.

OBSERVED BEHAVIORS

Hyperactive

Running back and forth into the living room

Arguing about every step of familiar bedtime routine

Loud, "bossy"

Seems really anxious about tornadoes and storms

POSSIBLE TRIGGERS/CIRCUMSTANCES

Happened at the end of a long day, lots of activity and people

Loud restaurant for dinner

Tornado season

This happens a lot at bedtime no matter what the day was like!

INTERVENTIONS

Develop a family routine for bedtime which includes Child's Pose (page 26) and (Legs Up the Wall (page 27)

Conductor Breath (page 44)—do this together with her

Slow Diaphragmatic Breathing (page 31)—buy a Hoberman sphere and practice together as a family

THE SNOWLINE

COGNITIVELY
The amygdala switches the brain into survival mode—the frontal lobe goes offline.

PHYSICALLY
We see the body responding to the survival mode though Flight/Fight/Freeze behaviors.

EMOTIONALLY
Because of survival mode, empathy, joy, and other feelings of connection cannot be accessed.

COGNITIVE

This is often the point at which we refer to kids as "gone" or "not there." And from a neurological perspective, that is actually somewhat true. As part of the stress response, the amygdala has gone into "survival mode" and has shut down a child's ability to reason, process information, and/or make decisions.

PHYSICAL

In Snowline, a child's brain has flooded her nervous system with adrenaline and cortisol. The muscle tension which started in Treeline has increased. A child will be experiencing strong fight/flight/freeze impulses, which might look like:

- Pacing
- Hiding (i.e., under a table or desk)
- Running away
- Attempting to throw punches, kick, or bite
- Swearing or other attempts to "punch" verbally

EMOTIONAL

It can't be emphasized enough that when in the Snowline zone, the child is in a full stress response, and the brain is only focusing on survival. Empathy (e.g., "think about how this makes someone else feel") is not available.

THE SNOWLINE

CASE STUDY: TANYA

Tanya is in math class, and the teacher announces there is a pop quiz on the last unit of material covered. Tanya's eyes widen and her cheeks flush, and she yells, "NO. WAY!" As the teacher hands out the blank quizzes to students, Tanya pulls her sweatshirt hood up and puts her head on her desk. The teacher asks her repeatedly to sit up, and then asks her if she needs help or a minute to sit outside to take a deep breath. Tanya is motionless and silent.

NOT YET IN THE SNOWLINE

The teacher turns away from Tanya, hands out the quiz to the other students, and then picks up a tin of sensory putty from the basket of fidgets on her desk. She quietly squats down next to Tanya and says, "It's okay, let's just do this for a minute and not think about the quiz."

Tanya reaches out a hand and starts squeezing and smashing the putty onto her desk. After a couple of minutes, she sits up again and is able to start work on her quiz. (Because Tanya is not able to talk but is able to respond to some releasing, sensory strategies practiced earlier, she is in Treeline.)

IN THE SNOWLINE

Frustrated by her lack of response, the teacher tells Tanya in a sharp tone that she will have to leave the classroom to "get it together." Tanya repeatedly screams obscenities at the teacher and at her classmates, also yelling, "DON'T LOOK AT ME!" and then slides underneath her desk. The teacher leans down to offer her putty, but she flings it across the room. Tanya curls up in a fetal position and for several minutes is completely unresponsive and shut down other than to scream or attempt to kick anyone who approaches her.

The teacher uses her walkie-talkie to call for a social worker, who comes quickly and leads the rest of the class out into the hall. The teacher then takes a couple of deep breaths, and at the same time does some shoulder rolls to open her chest. She then slowly sits down on the floor near Tanya, saying quietly, "I'm here, I get it, this is really tough, so I'm just going to hang out with you for a second." She sits quietly with her for a couple of minutes.

Gradually, Tanya begins moving around. She talks angrily about the quiz and the teacher nods and says, "Yep, I get it." She eventually crawls out from under the table and agrees to walk down the hall with the teacher to have "more time to calm down."

(Because Tanya is unable to respond to talking or to movement-based interventions, but is able to respond to a quiet, while the attuned adult provides safety and space to regulate, she is in Snowline.)

THE SNOWLINE

CASE STUDY: MICHAEL

Michael is engrossed in a chapter book when his fourth grade teacher states, "It is time to finish up in the next minute to get ready for recess." Michael continues reading, and the teacher states that the minute is up and to put everything away. The teacher notices Michael isn't stopping and asks him again to put down the book. Michael's face turns red and he slams the book down on the desk, yelling, "I HEARD you! I AM!"

NOT YET IN THE SNOWLINE

The teacher takes a slow inhale and exhale. She says, "Wow, Michael. You are really frustrated. It's so hard to stop when you want to keep going, isn't it?" Michael says, "YEAH!" and nods. The teacher says to the whole class, "Okay, everyone, before we go to recess, let's get our bodies ready by doing chair pushups!" The class is familiar with this, and all the children (including Michael) grab on to the seats of their chairs and push their bodies up using their arms. After three chair pushups, the teacher notices Michael taking a deep breath and making a joke to a friend.

(Because Michael is able to respond to body-based releasing techniques he learned while in Foothills, he is in Treeline.)

IN THE SNOWLINE

After throwing down his book, Michael tips over his desk and chair and runs out of the room swearing. He climbs into an open cubby in the hallway. The teacher runs out into the hallway, spots him, and says, "Okay, Michael, glad you're safe and someone will come help you." She then steps back into the room, slows down her breath, and radios for help. She immediately turns down one bank of lights in the room and acknowledges that "we all have difficult days" and invites the class to take some slow deep breaths with her.

The teacher asks the class if anyone else's heart rate just went up, stating that we all have different ways of expressing our emotions and that we affect each other. She asks if anyone wants to share what they do when they are frustrated or upset. In the meantime, a paraprofessional who knows Michael comes down the hall and sits quietly on the floor next to him as he huddles in the cubby. After a few minutes, Michael climbs out and accepts the paraprofessional's offer to go for a walk.

STRATEGIES THAT WORK

"The goal [of regulation] is to help children stay connected to themselves in the midst of their dysregulation so they can learn to feel it without becoming consumed by it." —Lisa Dion (See References.)

In Snowline, the helping adults don't just use interventions; we are the intervention. Because youth at this level of stress are in a fight/flight/freeze state and don't have access to their logical brain (Foothills) or their toolbox of regulation skills (Treeline), we shift out of those modes. Using our own nervous systems, we help youth feel safe enough to de-escalate by presencing, providing containment, and co-regulating.

Presencing

It may sound simple, but being present in a regulated, authentic way is actually the most important intervention we can provide for youth in Snowline. When a child's nervous system is highly activated, it is looking for anything that can stabilize it—especially a regulated adult's nervous system it can "borrow" for help.

Therefore, even if a child or youth can't hear our soothing words or utilize their own skills, us being authentically present as we work on being regulated is exactly the stabilizing force they need most. Of course, this is not always easy! Encountering Snowline triggers emotional and physical responses in our own bodies, so it is critical that we know how to "drop our energy" or "get grounded" so our nervous system can act as an anchor for the child. The more you practice how to stop right where you are, drop the energy into your feet and breathe, while keeping the upper body open with shoulders back and in, the more you will be able to access this skill.

- Being there: "Be where your feet are."

- Keeping the sense of "we" so the child does not feel alone in their pain.

- "Feeling felt" (D. Siegel, See Resources): Allow the child to know you "get it," you understand, your mind, body, and heart are fully present for them.

Example of Presencing

Next time you are in a frustrating situation, perhaps in a traffic jam, receiving startling news, try the following techniques. Memorize this like you have with the instructions for what to do if you catch on fire, "stop, drop, and roll." The same applies here, but don't roll, just stop, drop your energy into your feet, and breathe slowly.

Once you have stopped, do a quick body scan. To begin, release your jaw, soften your eyes, let your shoulders settle away from the ears, release your arms, and allow the palms to turn upward, allow your belly to soften, and begin to drop your breath down through your feet so you feel solid on the ground. Sometimes it helps to say the steps out loud as you are doing the release (soft jaw, soft eyes, etc.). What we are trying to do is unwind the nervous system from the top down. We want the upper body to be light, open, and at ease and the lower body (navel down) to be solid, sturdy, and grounded. This body form gives our brains the message of safety, containment, and openness. It shows how we can be stable and open. It allows us to show that we are here: mind, body, and heart.

Containment

In any time of escalation, our first concern is obviously to keep youth (and those around them) safe. Our first priority is to assess and address safety issues, and here are some tips to keep in mind while we do so:

Use the Presencing (page 54) and Co-regulation (page 57) strategies to set limits and take safety precautions in a mindful, regulated way versus being angry and reactive.

- Watch your language: keep talking to a minimum, but when necessary let the youth know what you are doing to keep them safe. Keep your voice calm and collaborative.

- Pre-planning: When possible, have conversations with youth about the plan for Snowline when they are not in Snowline and are calm enough to take in logic and ideas. This is never meant as a threat, but as a nurturing promise, e.g., "If you are super mad or having a meltdown, let's talk about the things I or other adults will do to keep you and everyone else safe. That way you know what to expect. Does that sound good to you?"

THE SNOWLINE

As mentioned in the Treeline section, "hacking" the vagus nerve to create a ventral vagal response is an extraordinarily powerful tool to decrease activation and increase engagement. However, no matter how helpful our directions or cues might be, children and youth in Snowline are not able to respond to them. In those situations, it is the adult who should activate their own ventral vagal response to become more regulated and authentically present. Once that happens, the child or youth will be able to "borrow" the adult's nervous system, which will allow them to feel safe and begin to de-escalate.

Examples of strategies for adults to use:
- Sitting on the ground, or if standing imagine you are pushing your feet into the floor and sending some of your tension out through the soles
- Drinking cold water (if it is possible and safe to leave the child/youth to go get some)
- Splashing cool/cold water on the face, ideally from the chin upwards (Dion, see Resources)
- Interlace your fingers and put gentle pressure on the top of your head
- Focus on your breathing. If you are breathing quickly using your chest, try dropping your attention to your belly and diaphragm and allow your exhalations to be twice as long as your inhalations.

Co-regulation

We provide co-regulation to intense and anxious youth in every Moving Mountains zone, but we do it differently in Snowline. As described earlier, because logic and verbal connection aren't available to youth in this zone, in order to de-escalate them we must 'lend' them our own nervous systems. Here are ways to do this:

- Be physically grounded and centered. Slow down breathing pattern; exhale twice as long as your inhale, and begin to bring awareness to the person next to you.

- Model breathing in a slow, rhythmic way. This is not the time that we are teaching children to slow down their breathing, but we are modeling it in our bodies.

- Possibly use aromatherapy. Have the student select smells that they like and perhaps have oils available to use if needed. Sometimes adults put the oils on their own hands.

WHAT ARE THE ADULTS DOING *DURING* SNOWLINE?

Be physically grounded and centered. Slow down breathing pattern: exhale twice as long as your inhale, and begin to bring awareness to the person next to you.

Once again drop "energy"/ground feet. Bring all your attention down to your feet. Allow your toes to spread and press the pads of your feet to the earth. Allow your energy to drop toward your feet. Take a few breaths into the feet and perhaps say to yourself, "I am here," or "I am grounded," or "I've got this."

It is also helpful to keep the upper body open, shoulders back and in, so your body is demonstrating the openness and presence which the young person in Snowline needs to pick up on in order to de-escalate.

WHAT ARE THE ADULTS DOING *AFTER* SNOWLINE?

See if you can release your jaw by yawning or looking away and sticking out your tongue. Perhaps do some shoulder rolls to release any tension in the neck and shoulders. Shake it off: Spend a minute shaking, swaying, doing a Forward Bend, or taking a very brisk walk.

SNOWLINE APPLICATION

These worksheets can be used as a tool to record your observations about behaviors and list possible interventions in the Snowline. Below, the sheets are filled out as if we were Tanya's teacher (or other school staff). The Appendix section of this manual contains reproducible application worksheets for you to copy and use in your work with the youth you know.

OBSERVED BEHAVIORS

Says "I'm tired" a lot, seems lethargic

Gets panicky

Screams and swears at me and her classmates

Shuts down (pulls her hood over her head, gets under her desk, fetal position)

Whipped the putty I offered her across the room

POSSIBLE TRIGGERS/CIRCUMSTANCES

Seems to always happen at test or time

Definitely worse when she is surprised, like a pop quiz

Fatigue? Parents say she gets enough sleep but not sure

INTERVENTIONS

First check with our own nervous system: body scan, where are we tense? (page 55)

Make our exhales twice as long as inhales

Roll shoulders a few times and release the neck

Check our tone of voice and keep talking to a minimum so she feels like we're there to help

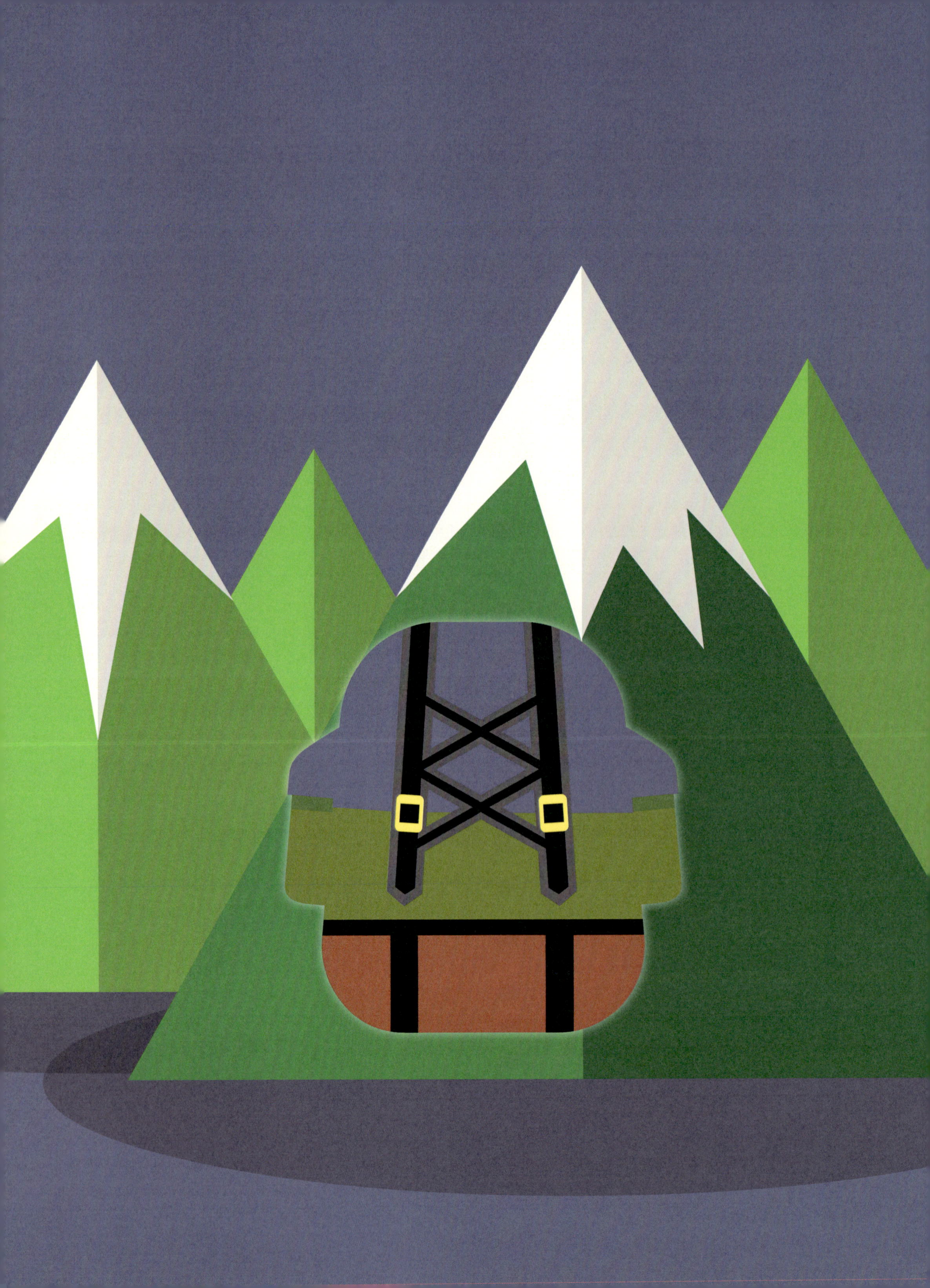

WHAT'S IN YOUR BACKPACK?

Any good mountain climber carries a backpack with the tools and other supplies they'll need on their journey. Some items are invaluable, but the climber may wish they could leave some others behind to lighten the load. Every one of us (children and adults) also has our own "backpack," which comes with us as we go up and down the mountain of stress and activation.

Each backpack is a unique combination of temperament, sensory thresholds, and other traits that make us who we are. As with a real climbing pack, some of those traits can be very useful, and some can be difficult.

As we've stressed, the most important self-regulation tools that anxious and reactive children and adolescents possess are the relationships they have with caring adults. To be the best possible partner for young people in distress, we need to know the contents of our own "backpack," including:

- Ways that feelings manifests in our body
- Sensory thresholds and calming strategies
- Temperament traits

Being familiar with our "backpack" helps us:

- Be more aware of our own reactions.
- Be more intentional about regulating our stress.
- Increase our ability to be present for the children we are supporting.

Moving Mountains Manual

YOUR BACKPACK

HOW TO USE THIS SECTION

1

Fill out the worksheets in this section for yourself. See if you learn anything new!

2

Think of an emotionally reactive child you work with or parent. Fill out the sheets again, this time from the point of view of that child. You might not have all the information, but do your best with what you do know.

3

Compare your results with the child's results. Can you notice ways in which the two of you are similar? Reflect on how this might affect your relationship and your work together.

Please note: reproducible versions of these worksheets are also available in the Appendix.

Moving Mountains Manual

YOUR BACKPACK

FEELINGS IN THE BODY

You may already be a believer in the connection between our emotions and our bodies. However, not everyone is identical in the ways stress and strong emotions manifest physically.

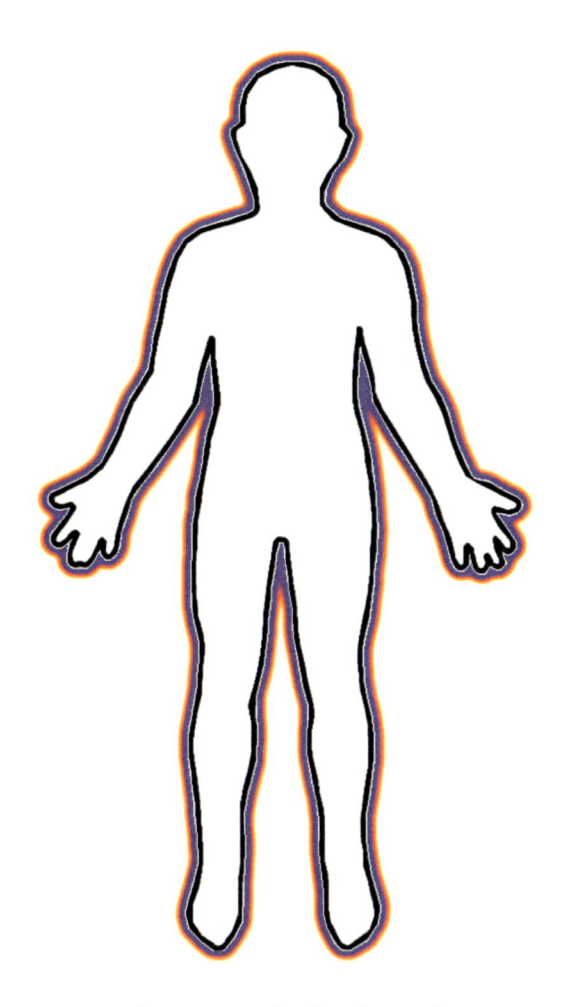

We feel stress just as much in our bodies as in our minds. Using the body outline, label and describe what physical sensations are signals that you are stressed.

Everybody is different, but here are some examples:

- Tightness or squeezing in the chest
- Flushed or hot face
- "Buzzy" feeling in the mind
- Racing heart
- Tense shoulders
- Etc.

Moving Mountains Manual

YOUR BACKPACK

There is a difference between being with children while they are in their discomfort, feeling the discomfort, and regulating alongside them, versus wanting to rescue the children out of their discomfort because we either believe that it isn't OK for them to be uncomfortable or we are too uncomfortable. . . . The first is integrative. The second is avoidance.—Lisa Dion [See References]

An important part of your "backpack" is your own history with explosive or reactive behavior. Over the course of your lives, what lessons were you taught about how children and youth should manage their emotions and behaviors? And what were you taught about how adults should respond to them? Awareness of these lessons helps you sort out which ideas are still useful, and which ones you might want to gently remove from our backpacks as we move forward.

Questions to consider

When I was growing up, how did adults respond to a child who was having an outburst? What words did they use? How did they react physically? *What parts of this do I still think are helpful? What parts have I let go of?*

How old do I think children/youth need to be before they can "control" their behavior, and if they can't at that age why does that happen? *Have my answers to these questions changed at any point in my life?*

When I was growing up, was it safe for me to express big emotions like fear and anger? What were some of the ways adults responded to me when I did? *What helped me? What did not help me?*

- When a child/youth I'm with is in Treeline or Snowline, what are some of the feelings and thoughts I'm noticing myself having? *Are there friends, colleagues, and other people I can share these feelings with?*

- Examples of feelings: anger, fatigue, powerlessness, annoyance, compassion, confusion

- Examples of thoughts: "Oh no," "Yikes, this is scary," "Not again," "OK, let's figure this out."

"I AM HERE."
"I AM GROUNDED."
"I'VE GOT THIS."

YOUR BACKPACK

SENSORY THRESHOLDS PART I:

THINGS THAT BUG US

As mentioned before, we are constantly awash in sensory input. Adults as well as children have sensory "thresholds" that impact self-regulation. For example, let's say you hate the glare and buzz of fluorescent lights. And let's say you happen to work in a public school building that is full of those lights! This means you are coping with highly unpleasant sensory input all day, and as soon as you walk in the door in the morning you will already have started your climb through the Foothills of your stress mountain.

Use the worksheet on page 67.

SENSORY THRESHOLDS PART I: THINGS THAT BUG US

Circle words or phrases that bother, bug, irrationally irritate, stress, annoy, or make you nuts!

Uncomfortable clothes
   (tags, itchiness, heavy snow clothes, boots)
Bright lights
Having to sit still for long periods of time
Certain noises
   (crinkling paper, nails on a chalkboard)

Certain smells (which ones?)
Small, cramped spaces
Being hot or cold
Big crowds
Quiet rooms
Loud music

Create your own list

YOUR BACKPACK

SENSORY THRESHOLDS: PART II

THINGS THAT SOOTHE US

Seeking the right kind of sensory input can also be one of the most powerful ways to feel grounded and calm. As with sensory thresholds, we are each unique in terms of what types of input work best for us.

Use the worksheet on page 69.

SENSORY THRESHOLDS PART II: THINGS THAT SOOTHE US

Circle words or phrases that calm, mellow, soothe, relax, help, or chill you out.

Having something to do with your hands
Wrapping up in a shawl, blanket, sweater
Somewhere quiet
Sucking on hard candy or chewing gum
Sleeping
Music

Time alone
Moving around (jumping, dancing)
Favorite smells (list)
Quiet rooms
Sitting in a rocking chair

Create your own list

_____
_____
_____
_____
_____
_____
_____
_____
_____
_____
_____
_____
_____
_____
_____
_____
_____

YOUR BACKPACK

TEMPERAMENT

"Temperament" refers to the idea that human beings have certain differences in personality that are innate. As noted earlier, the answer to "Nature vs. Nature?" is "Yes!" And we as humans are deeply influenced by our environments and relationships. However, temperament refers to certain things about us that are just part of who we are, and who we have been since birth. Chess and Thomas (*See* Glossary) identified certain elements of temperament, including activity level, rhythmicity, being an introvert or extrovert, adaptability, and intensity. Use this sheet to reflect on the characteristics of some of the children you work with or know. Then reflect on your own characteristics! Children are not always a perfect "temperamental fit" with their environments or with the adults they know, and awareness of fit can make it easier to think creatively about how and where support is needed.

SELF-ASSESSMENT: WHAT'S IN YOUR BACKPACK?

ACTIVITY LEVEL
Indicate the number that represents your temperament.

1 2 3 4 5

Your body simply feels better if it is at rest. Having to move around a lot is tiring and discombobulating. If you can be quiet and at rest, you feel at ease.

Your body simply feels better if it is in motion. Sitting still makes you uncomfortable, but if you can move, you feel better.

RHYTHMICITY
Indicate the number that represents your temperament.

1 2 3 4 5

Left to your own devices you like to "wing it." Your biological systems (sleeping, appetite, digestive issues) are easily knocked off kilter by unusual events, stresses or changes and when this happens it impacts you a great deal.

Your appetite and ability to sleep the same amount each night are relatively unchanged by stress. Left to your own devices you would keep the same bedtimes and mealtimes every day.

INTROVERT/EXTROVERT
Indicate the number that represents your temperament.

1 2 3 4 5

When you are really happy OR really stressed, what helps you the most is to spend time alone until your system feels rebalanced and you have processed your feelings. After that, you are ready to spend time with people again.

When you are really happy OR really stressed, what helps you the most is to reach out immediately to other people to get comfort, vent, or process. Doing this balances your system and after that you are ready to relax by yourself.

ADAPTABILITY
Indicate the number that represents your temperament.

1 2 3 4 5

Although you try, you don't like change. Even if your logical mind is perfectly fine with changes in routines, expectations, or people, you react strongly to them.

You love change and can switch gears immediately.

INTENSITY
Indicate the number that represents your temperament.

1 2 3 4 5

Happy, sad, or stressful, your reactions to situations are not particularly strong. You are described as "even-keeled."

Happy, sad, or stressful, your reactions to situations are quite strong. Your mood shifts frequently.

SNOWLINE

TREELINE

FOOTHILLS

CONCLUSION

Thank you for taking the opportunity to learn about Moving Mountains, a metaphor for illustrating the "zones" of escalation in the brain and nervous system. Hopefully you've had a chance to reflect on the youth with intensity, reactivity, and anxiety, you know, as well as on your own, needs as a caregiver. This framework can serve as an organizational system to "file" and evaluate useful interventions, as well as the additional tools and strategies included within each zone.

Now consider what impact using this manual will have on you and your work with children. We are hopeful that you will experience at least some of the positive changes that developing the Moving Mountains framework brought to our own practices, which have included:

IMPROVEMENT
in our sense of effectiveness with some of the most difficult-to-manage behaviors and issues.

CREATION
of new opportunities for healing, learning, and connection between ourselves and the children who need our help.

ESTABLISHMENT
of a new relationship with self-care. "Self-care" has become a widely used term for anything enjoyable or healthy we do to replenish ourselves.

UNDERSTANDING
our own nervous system, emotions, and sensory thresholds help us create more efficient self-care. Just as with the children we know, the experiences that we need to regulate and replenish can differ widely day to day based on what experiences we have had and what zones of the "mountain" we've climbed to!

CONCLUSION

WHAT ARE THE NEXT STEPS:

Consider the next steps needed to implement the Moving Mountains framework:

1. Mindful observation
Continue to regularly check in on yourself and the children you know and work with. Notice what zones of activation you and they are in throughout the day, and observe what is working well and what is hard. This kind of mindful observation often works best when you can regularly set aside a small amount of time (even just a few moments) to talk with a coworker or friend, write down some thoughts, or even sit quietly in the car to collect your thoughts.

_____
_____

2. Self-care
What changes will you make for yourself to help your own self-regulation and replenishment? What activities might you try or do more of?

_____
_____
_____
_____
_____

3. Changes to your work with children
What are some new ideas you might plan to try? Examples: change how you interpret certain behaviors, identify new practices and strategies to teach youth in the Foothills, advocate for changes in your workplace environment to make it more regulating, etc.

_____
_____
_____
_____
_____

4. Use *Moving Mountains* as a filing system
In the next section, we offer an opportunity for you to "file" the wonderful interventions you know into the right zones. As you learn new strategies, use the reproducible sheets to keep organizing them.

APPENDICES

GLOSSARY

BIBLIOGRAPHY, RESOURCES

WORKSHEETS

GLOSSARY

ADHD/ADD (attention deficit disorder with/without hyperactivity). This is one of the most commonly diagnosed mental health diagnoses for children/teens who often exhibit impulsivity, difficulty paying attention, disorganization. Grief, anxiety, and trauma often present similarly to ADHD or ADD.

Anxiety. A state of being characterized by feelings of tension, worried thoughts, and physical changes. Anxiety is a normal part of being human but, when extreme or chronic, can result in mental health diagnoses and other issues.

APA. American Psychological Association.

Arousal. State of being physiologically alert or awake.

ASD (autism spectrum disorder). The criteria for this diagnosis include difficulty with social communication, stereotyped or rigid interests and other behaviors.

Complex trauma. Also called "developmental trauma disorder" (Van der Kolk, 2005). Consists of experiences of multiple traumas, often within a child's caregiving system, rooted in early life experiences; and responsible for emotional, behavioral, cognitive, and meaning-making disturbances.

Diaphragmatic breathing. Deep breathing that begins by contracting the diaphragm. Air enters the lungs and expands chest and belly. When one inhales, the diaphragm lowers and pushes out the belly. (Why we call this "belly" breathing.)

Depression.
A state of being including sadness, irritability, and/or agitation, lack of interest in pleasurable activities, and physical changes to sleep, appetite. Depression can be temporary and situational or chronic and severe.

Developmental equifinality.
Different experiences in childhood can lead to the same developmental result (Cicchetti and Toth, 2013).

GLOSSARY

Emotional regulation.
The ability to increase or decrease responses in order to stay within a tolerable (to self and others) range of feelings.

Co-regulation.
When one person works directly to emotionally regulate another person. Usually we think of adults regulating children, but adults co-regulate with each other all the time!

Self-regulation.
The ability to regulate one's own emotions without the direct help of another person. We learn this set of skills by internalizing the co-regulation we receive from others.

Mindfulness.
"Paying attention in a particular way: on purpose, in the present moment and non-judgmentally," according to Jon Kabat-Zinn, University of Massachusetts Medical Center emeritus professor of Medicine, who developed Mindfulness-Based Stress Reduction classes (MBSR). Mindfulness practices have been around for more than 5,000 years. Mindfulness and yoga-based practices have shown to reduce anxiety, improve gross motor development, increase attention span, improve mood.

Neuroscience.
Neuroscience focuses on the structure and function of the nervous system and brain in relation to behavior and learning. (One of the most powerful ways to frame "behavior" is to have youth understand the brain/body connection.)

Parasympathetic nervous system.
One of the three main branches of the autonomic nervous system, often referred to as the "rest and digest" system. It slows the heart rate, respiration, and blood pressure. With youth, we sometimes call this system "the brakes."

Sensory threshold.
The ability to process and make sense of multiple sources of sensory input (e.g., what is being received through visual, auditory, tactile, etc., channels). Difficulties with sensory integration can cause significant anxiety and overwhelm children and adults.

Sympathetic nervous system.
One of the three main branches of the autonomic nervous system. The sympathetic nervous system makes the body ready for fight/flight/freeze and is responsible for the acceleration of the heart rate and respiration and raising blood pressure. With youth, we sometimes call this system "the accelerator."

GLOSSARY

Temperament.
Innate characteristics (e.g., intensity level, rhythmicity, etc.) present from birth (Chess and Thomas, 1996).

Trauma.
A experience which is threatening to one's wellbeing or that of others and which overwhelms our ability to cope or respond. The two primary types of trauma are complex trauma (see earlier entry) and single event trauma.

Triggers.
Actions or experiences that initiate or precipitate an emotional or physical response. A negative emotional response can be sadness, grief, anger, fear. Individuals can be "triggered" by sensory input (taste, touch, smell, sights, and sounds).

BIBLIOGRAPHY, RESOURCES

Books

Allen, J., and R. Klein. *Ready . . . Set . . . R.E.L.A.X.: A Research-Based Program of Relaxation, Learning, and Self-Esteem for Children.* United States: Inner Coaching, 1997.

———. *RELAX Calm: Helping Teens Manage Stress Using Relaxation & Guided Imagery.* United States: Inner Coaching, 2011.

Chess, S., and A. Thomas. *Temperament: Theory and Practice.* United States: Routledge, 1996.

Cichetti, D., and F. Rogosch. Equifinality and Multifinality in Developmental Psychopathology. *Development and Psychopathology,* 8 (597–600), 1996.

Cohen, L. *The Opposite of Worry: The Playful Parenting Approach to Childhood Anxieties and Fears.* New York: Ballantine, 2013.

Dana, D. *A Beginner's Guide to Polyvagal Theory,* Retrieved from https://www.rhythmofregulation.com/resources/Beginner's%20Guide.pdf, 2018.

Dion, L. *Aggression In Play Therapy: A Neurobiological Approach for Integrating Intensity.* New York: W.W. Norton, 2018.

———. *Aggression In the Playroom: A Synergetic Approach for Working with Trauma and Intensity in Play Therapy.* Presented at the conference of the Minnesota Association for Play Therapy, Eagan, Minnesota, 2020.

Emerson, D. and E. Hopper. *Overcoming Trauma Through Yoga.* United States: North Atlantic, 2011.

Gearity, A. *Developmental Repair: A Training Manual.* Retrieved from https://washburn.org/wp-content/uploads/2015/07/WCCDevRepair-revised.pdf, 2015.

Gillen, Lynea, and James Gillen. *Yoga Calm for Children: Educating Heart, Mind, and Body.* United States: Three Pebbles Press, LLC, 2007.

Jensen, E. *Teaching With the Brain In Mind.* United States: Association for Supervision and Curriculum Development (ASCD), 2005.

Levine, P. *Healing Trauma.* Boulder, Colorado: Sounds True, 2005.

———. *Waking the Tiger: Healing Trauma.* United States: North Atlantic, 1997.

Menakem, Resmaa. *My Grandmother's Hands: Racialized Trauma and the Pathway to Mending Our Hearts and Bodies.* Central Recovery, 2017.

Nagoski, A., and E. Nagoski. *Burnout: Secrets to Unlocking the Stress Cycle.* United States: Ballantine, 2019.

Porges, S., and D. Dana, eds. *Clinical Applications of the Polyvagal Theory.* New York: W.W. Norton, 2018.

Sapolsky, R. *Why Zebras Don't Get Ulcers.* New York: Henry Holt, 1998.

Siegel, D. *The Mindful Brain.* United States: Mind Your Brain, Inc., 2007.

———. *Brain Storm: The Power and Purpose of the Teenage Brain.* United States: Penguin, 2013.

Siegel, D., and T. Payne Bryson. T*he Whole-Brain Child: 12 Revolutionary Strategies to Nurture Your Child's Developing Mind.* New York: Delacorte, 2011.

———. *No-Drama Discipline: The Whole-Brain Way to Calm the Chaos and Nurture Your Child's Developing Mind.* New York: Bantam, 2016.

Van der Kolk, B. *The Body Keeps the Score: Brain, Mind, and Body in the Healing of Trauma.* New York: Penguin, 2014.

BIBLIOGRAPHY, RESOURCES

Research to support the use of Yoga-Based Movement with youth

Beauchemin, J., Hutchins, T. L., & Patterson, F. (2008). Mindfulness meditation may lessen anxiety, promote social skills, and improve academic performance among adolescents with learning disabilities. *Complementary Health Practice Review,* 13(1), 34–45.

Butzer, B., Bury, D., Telles, S., and Khalsa, S. (2016). Implementing yoga within the school curriculum: a scientific rationale for improving social-emotional learning and positive student outcomes, *Journal of Children's Services,* Vol. 11 No. 1, 3–24. https://doi. org/10.1108/JCS-10-2014-0044.

Butzer, B., Day, D., Potts, A., Ryan, C., Coulombe, S., Davies, B., and Khalsa, S.B.S. (2015). Effects of a classroom-based yoga intervention on cortisol and behavior in second- and third-grade students. A pilot study. *Journal of Evidence-Based Complementary & Alternative Medicine,* 20, 41–49.

Daly, L. A., Haden, S. C., Hagins, M., Papouchis, N., and Ramirez, P. M. (2015). Yoga and emotion regulation in high school students: A randomized controlled trial. *Evidence-Based Complementary and Alternative Medicine.*

Fishbein, D., Miller, S., Herman-Stahl, M., Williams, J., Lavery, B., Markovitz, L., and Johnson, M. (2016). Behavioral and psychophysiological effects of a yoga intervention on high-risk adolescents: A randomized control trial. *Journal of Child and Family Studies,* 25(2), 518–529.

Jensen, P.S., and Kenny, D.T. (2004). The effects of yoga on the attention and behavior of boys with attention-deficit/hyperactivity disorder (ADHD). *Journal of Attention Disorders,* 7(4), 205–216.

Kauts, A., and Sharma, N. (2009). Effect of yoga on academic performance in relation to stress. *International Journal of Yoga,* 2(1), 39.

Napoli, M., Krech, P.R., and Holley, L.C. (2005). Mindfulness training for elementary school students: The attention academy. *Journal of applied school psychology,* 21(1), 99–125.

Schonert-Reichl, K.A., and Lawlor, M.S. (2010). The effects of a mindfulness-based education program on pre-and early adolescents' well-being and social and emotional competence. *Mindfulness,* 1(3), 137–151.

FOR MOVEMINDFULLY® PRODUCTS GO TO:
https://move-mindfully.com/store

FOR INFORMATION ON MOVING MOUNTAINS TRAININGS, CONSULTATIONS, AND PRODUCTS GO TO:
https://move-mindfully.com/MovingMountains

WORKSHEETS

You may reproduce any of the worksheets on the following pages with our permission. Use them to do good in the world.

ENVIRONMENTAL PATHWAYS QUESTIONS

What environmental stressors are the children you work with experiencing?

_____

_____

What are the stressors in your community?

_____

_____

How do these community stressors impact you personally?

_____

_____

INTERNAL/ORGANIC PATHWAYS QUESTIONS

What are the common internal/organic issues or diagnoses you observe in the children and youth you work with?

_____

_____

How do these issues impact your relationship with these children?

_____

_____

What internal/organic issues or diagnoses do you yourself struggle with?

_____

_____

FOOTHILLS APPLICATION

Use this page as a tool to record your observations about behaviors, and list possible interventions to use in the Foothills.

OBSERVED BEHAVIORS

_____

_____

_____

_____

_____

POSSIBLE TRIGGERS/CIRCUMSTANCES

_____

_____

_____

_____

_____

INTERVENTIONS

_____

_____

_____

_____

_____

TREELINE APPLICATION

Use this page as a tool to record your observations about behaviors, and list possible interventions to use in the Treeline.

OBSERVED BEHAVIORS

_____

_____

_____

_____

POSSIBLE TRIGGERS/CIRCUMSTANCES

_____

_____

_____

_____

INTERVENTIONS

_____

_____

_____

_____

SNOWLINE APPLICATION

Use this page as a tool to record your observations about behaviors, and list possible interventions to use in the Snowline.

OBSERVED BEHAVIORS

_____

_____

_____

_____

POSSIBLE TRIGGERS/CIRCUMSTANCES

_____

_____

_____

_____

INTERVENTIONS

_____

_____

_____

_____

SENSORY THRESHOLDS PART I: THINGS THAT BUG US

Circle words or phrases that bother, bug, irrationally irritate, stress, annoy, or make you nuts!

Uncomfortable clothes
   (tags, itchiness, heavy snow clothes, boots)
Bright lights
Having to sit still for long periods of time
Certain noises
   (crinkling paper, nails on a chalkboard)

Certain smells (which ones?)
Small, cramped spaces
Being hot or cold
Big crowds
Quiet rooms
Loud music

Create your own list

_____
_____
_____
_____
_____
_____
_____
_____
_____
_____
_____
_____
_____
_____
_____
_____
_____
_____
_____
_____

SENSORY THRESHOLDS PART II: THINGS THAT SOOTHE US

Circle words or phrases that calm, mellow, soothe, relax, help, or chill you out.

Having something to do with your hands
Wrapping up in a shawl, blanket, sweater
Somewhere quiet
Sucking on hard candy or chewing gum
Sleeping
Music

Time alone
Moving around (jumping, dancing)
Favorite smells (list)
Quiet rooms
Sitting in a rocking chair

Create your own list

SELF-ASSESSMENT: WHAT'S IN YOUR BACKPACK?

ACTIVITY LEVEL
Indicate the number that represents your temperament.

1   2   3   4   5

Your body simply feels better if it is at rest. Having to move around a lot is tiring and discombobulating. If you can be quiet and at rest, you feel at ease.	Your body simply feels better if it is in motion. Sitting still makes you uncomfortable, but if you can move, you feel better.

RHYTHMICITY
Indicate the number that represents your temperament.

1   2   3   4   5

Left to your own devices you like to "wing it." Your biological systems (sleeping, appetite, digestive issues) are easily knocked off kilter by unusual events, stresses or changes and when this happens it impacts you a great deal.	Your appetite and ability to sleep the same amount each night are relatively unchanged by stress. Left to your own devices you would keep the same bedtimes and mealtimes every day.

INTROVERT/EXTROVERT
Indicate the number that represents your temperament.

1   2   3   4   5

When you are really happy OR really stressed, what helps you the most is to spend time alone until your system feels rebalanced and you have processed your feelings. After that, you are ready to spend time with people again.	When you are really happy OR really stressed, what helps you the most is to reach out immediately to other people to get comfort, vent, or process. Doing this balances your system and after that you are ready to relax by yourself.

ADAPTABILITY
Indicate the number that represents your temperament.

1   2   3   4   5

Although you try, you don't like change. Even if your logical mind is perfectly fine with changes in routines, expectations or people, you react strongly to them. Eventually you . . .	You love change and can switch gears immediately.

INTENSITY
Indicate the number that represents your temperament.

1   2   3   4   5

Happy, sad, or stressful, your reactions to situations are not particularly strong. You are described as "even-keeled."	Happy, sad, or stressful, your reactions to situations are quite strong. Your mood shifts frequently.

FEELINGS IN THE BODY

You may already be a believer in the connection between our emotions and our bodies. However, not everyone is identical in the ways stress and strong emotions manifest physically.

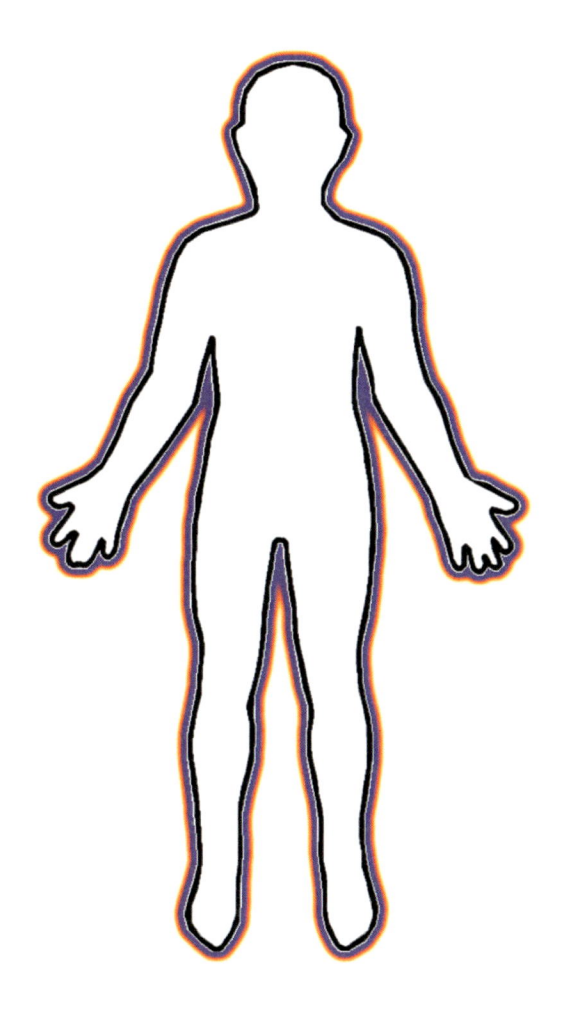

We feel stress just as much in our bodies as in our minds. Using the body outline, label and describe what physical sensations are signals that you are stressed.

Everybody is different, but here are some examples:

- Tightness or squeezing in the chest
- Flushed or hot face
- "Buzzy" feeling in the mind
- Racing heart
- Tense shoulders
- Etc.

©2020, Kathy Flaminio and Marit Appeldoorn — Moving Mountains Manual

WHO WE ARE

MARIT

Marit Appeldoorn, MSW, LICSW, RPT-S is a psychotherapist and registered play therapist supervisor in private practice in Minneapolis, Minnesota. She holds a master's degree in clinical social work from Smith College, and has twenty-five years of experience providing mental health care to distressed children and families. Marit completed Yoga Calm© certification and training in Somatic Experiencing™ and Theraplay®, and specializes in integrative approaches to healing and enhancing parent-child relationships. She is on the adjunct faculty of Augsburg University and St. Mary's University and is a co-founder of Safe Haven, an organization providing comprehensive professional support to therapists including supervision, training, mentorship, and coaching.

KATHY

Kathy Flaminio, LGSW, MSW, E-RYT-200, is the founder of MoveMindfully® a training and consulting company that brings the science of mindfulness, movement, and social-emotional learning into educational, therapeutic, and home environments. She is the creator of MoveMindfully trainings, workshops, products, and curriculum that teach trauma-responsive, practices for self-regulation, focus, and overall well-being. Kathy holds a master's degree in social work with twenty years of experience in Minneapolis Public Schools. She is a registered yoga teacher and certified Yoga Calm® master trainer. Kathy offers graduate level accredited courses, and has trained over 50,000 professionals in yoga-based movement, mindfulness, and social/emotional skills for use in classrooms, hospitals, home care, juvenile service centers, and therapeutic settings. Kathy has partnered with the University of Minnesota Masonic Children's Hospital and United Hospital to provide trauma-responsive practices to the child/adolescent and adult mental health units. She co-authored the Teen Resiliency Program with Dr. Henry Emmons along with other physicians and psychologists. This program is an integrative skill-based model used to support teens with anxiety, depression, and other stress-related conditions.